Tyler Perry: Interviews

Conversations with Filmmakers Series
Gerald Peary, General Editor

Tyler Perry
INTERVIEWS

Edited by Janice D. Hamlet

University Press of Mississippi / Jackson

The University Press of Mississippi is the scholarly publishing agency of
the Mississippi Institutions of Higher Learning: Alcorn State University,
Delta State University, Jackson State University, Mississippi State University,
Mississippi University for Women, Mississippi Valley State University,
University of Mississippi, and University of Southern Mississippi.

www.upress.state.ms.us

The University Press of Mississippi is a member of the Association of University Presses.

First printing 2019
∞

Library of Congress Control Number: 2019945843
Hardcover 978-1-4968-2458-5
Trade paperback 978-1-4968-2459-2
Epub single 978-1-4968-2460-8
Epub institutional 978-1-4968-2457-8
PDF single 978-1-4968-2461-5
PDF institutional 978-1-4968-2462-2

British Library Cataloging-in-Publication Data available

Contents

Introduction

I first heard of Tyler Perry in 2002 from a student in my undergraduate rhetorical criticism class. The student approached me after class following my discussion of their first writing assignment. She asked if she could do her critical analysis on a play she had recently seen performed. A new African American playwright had written the play. His name was Tyler Perry. She asked if I had heard of him. I replied, "No." After responding, I attempted to discourage her from selecting the play for critical analysis by reminding her that the process of rhetorical criticism requires a close reading of a text, employing a critical examination of the interactions between text, author and audience. To successfully accomplish this task requires that the critic read the text more than once. Trying to analyze a live performance based solely on memory would make the analysis difficult to accomplish. The student informed me that she did not merely see the performance but was able to acquire an underground copy of it on DVD. She talked about how the play was funny and culturally relevant and how this playwright was going to be famous once mainstream America discovered him. Therefore, I exhaled and said, "Okay. Let's see what you do with it." The rhetorical analysis was of Perry's third play, *I Can Do Bad All by Myself*. The play was about a woman fighting to hold on to her husband after she was served with divorce papers. She is unaware that her husband has moved in with one of her sisters and they are planning to marry. In her despair, the woman moves in with her grandmother who had just gotten out of the hospital. Also living with her grandmother is another sister and her daughter. A young man who was recently released from jail and does odd jobs around the house also lives with the grandmother. Lastly, the grandmother's daughter comes home for a visit. Because of all of the people living in this house and the various interactions that occurr, the woman comes to the realization that her hurt and other frustrations have consumed most of her life and she needs a change. The lesson presented through this morality play is "We fight so hard to hold on to the things that God, Himself, is trying to tear apart." Interestingly, instead of focusing on one or all of the sisters in the story, my student chose to focus on the grandmother, the matriarch of the family, an elderly trash-talking woman affectionately known as Madea. Throughout the play, Madea offers homespun solutions to everyone's problems. The student's analysis was actually good and quite informative. From reading her paper, I was introduced to Tyler Perry, the playwright. Now, some sixteen years later, my former student would likely find it amusing to discover that her former professor now owns a DVD collection of Tyler Perry's stage plays and films and has edited a collection of his interviews.

Once destitute and struggling for recognition as a playwright, Tyler Perry is now a multimedia phenomenon. Playwright, songwriter, screenwriter, producer, executive producer, director, actor, author, studio proprietor, and philanthropist, Perry has become one of the most lucrative auteurs in Hollywood, although he lives and works far from it. Perry's feature films have earned more than $500 million at the box office with an average opening-weekend gross of $25 million. This is a major accomplishment for any filmmaker but especially significant for an African American filmmaker whose films consist of mostly African American cast members. Perry credits his success, in part, to African Americans, especially African American religious women who have largely patronized his stage plays followed by his films. Therefore, Perry came to the risky business of filmmaking having already secured a loyal African American fan base nationwide through his stage plays. Consequently, this patronage allowed Perry to develop an unwavering, uncompromising, albeit audacious rhetorical style to his media creations which he writes, directs, and produces. These media creations feature social and cultural themes centered on faith, family, forgiveness, and overcoming adversity. Characters ungrudgingly implore religious and spiritual expressions in both discourse and song. Women are always at the center of the stories. Although consumers of his productions often criticize Perry for being predictable because he repeats themes and characterizations, he argues that the repetition of themes and characters is intentional because it is part of the Tyler Perry brand. A significant part of the Tyler Perry brand consists of drama and comedy laced with oral lessons trumpeting Christianity and personal accountability. He uses biblical satires to celebrate Christian culture within the comedic context of secular movies.

As a result of his childhood experiences, struggles to become known, and now his recognition as one of America's most successful auteurs, Tyler Perry has become a sought-after guest on numerous radio and television talk shows, in print newspapers and magazines, and on internet sites. Questions frequently asked in interviews fall into one or more of the following categories: Perry's abusive childhood and the power of forgiveness; Perry's rags to riches story; the birth and popularity of Perry's most profitable character, Madea; the Tyler Perry Studios; responses to critics; and the promotion of upcoming movies, whether ones he created or those created by others in which he has a starring role.

Tyler Perry, named Emmitt Perry Jr., was born on September 14, 1969, in New Orleans, Louisiana. Often the recipient of his father's rage, Perry encountered frequent physical, verbal, and emotional abuse throughout his childhood. Perry has informed some of his interviewers that he often took refuge in the crawlspace of his childhood house to escape his father. His only comfort was his mother who would take him to church on Sundays. As a participant in his community's African American church, Perry's artistic career combining electrifying gospel music with theatricality did not begin with his plays but as a young member of a church choir. Perry discovered early in his life that religion could be not only spiritual but entertaining as well. As a result, he infused African American worship practices into many of his stage plays, films, and television shows, accompanied by the energetic gospel traditions he had enjoyed in church. Perry frequently tells audiences that these experiences resulted in an empire grounded in Christian messages that focus on the challenges, aspirations, and, sometimes, eccentricities of church-going African Americans but whose storylines can be appreciated by a global audience.

Tyler Perry was in his late teens when, watching a segment of *The Oprah Winfrey Show*, he was inspired to start writing. Hearing someone on the show say that writing about your experiences and feelings was cathartic, he started journaling. However, to protect his identity, Perry wrote down his feelings in the form of letters in case someone discovered the journals. This journaling activity proved to be a very important component in Perry's development and subsequent success as a playwright and filmmaker.

These letters later served as the basis for Perry's first play, a musical titled, *I Know I've Been Changed*. The musical focused on two adult survivors of child abuse who became the very people that their abusive mothers predicted they would become. In 1992, he decided to launch a stage production of the play. It premiered in 1993 and was a dramatic and financial flop. Only thirty people showed up for the play's first weekend run. Nevertheless, Perry refused to give up. He found investors and took the play on the road, touring small venues and theaters throughout Georgia and other cities in the South for five years. Despite movement and financial support, the play continued to flop, and resources dwindled. Years passed. Perry lost the means to support himself and ended up living on the streets for three months.

By 1998, Perry's state of being changed. First, he found the courage to forgive his father for his years of abuse as he came to understand that forgiveness is not for the person who hurt you but for yourself so you can move on with your life. Perry reveals to the interviewers that his relationship with his father is why forgiveness is a salient theme in his artistry. He works out the pains of his childhood and the demons of his past through his art offering pragmatic assets that many moviegoers find useful toward negotiating their own tragedies and disappointments.

Later, after several attempts to stage his play, making revisions along the way, he arranged for what he thought would be a final run at the House of Blues in

Atlanta. However, the play miraculously sold out eight times. Two weeks later, the performance moved to the Fox Theatre in Atlanta where nearly 9,000 people attended during its run. Subsequently, the creation and production of other plays followed. Perry also visited many of Atlanta's African American churches, becoming a spokesperson for his plays and the values it communicated. His play, he made clear, delivered a Christian message. Perry also made his plays accessible through professionally recorded home videos, leading to the creation of an underground fan base.

Following the success of his plays, movies became the logical next step for Perry, which introduced him to the world of Hollywood politics, procedures, and processes. Perry often informs interviewers that when he made the rounds at major film studios to pitch film projects based on his morality plays, executives did not know what to make of him and were not interested in his projects. Perry takes a certain pleasure in telling interviewers how he was stunned by one executive explaining to him that churchgoing African Americans do not go to movies. Perry set out to prove him wrong. What happened next made Hollywood react. Perry found a cofinancier in Lionsgate Productions and his first play-turned-film, *Diary of a Mad Black Woman*, opened in February 2005. The film grossed over $50 million. Its audience was predominantly African American. Almost a year after *Diary of a Mad Black Woman*'s debut, Perry released his second feature film, *Madea's Family Reunion*. The film debuted as that weekend's top-grossing movie, taking in $30 million. Perry's ability to connect with largely African American audiences as evident in his successful plays eventually secured him a national following when he ventured into film and proved to be more relevant to his cinematic entrance and success. For this reason, Tyler Perry came to the perilous and costly field of filmmaking having already secured a loyal African American fan base nationwide through his plays.

Having shown that African American churchgoers are also filmgoers, Perry set out to introduce himself to mainstream America. With *Madea's Family Reunion*, which Perry wrote, directed, produced, and starred in (playing multiple roles), he got Hollywood's attention and approval. Lionsgate, the studio that cofinanced and distributed *Diary of a Mad Black Woman*, financed *Madea's Family Reunion*. Perry and Lionsgate soon after became partners. Most of Perry's movies are adapted from a storyline in his stage productions. For example, the storyline in *I Can Do Bad All by Myself* is quite different from the storyline in the movie version. Perry allows the storyline to deviate artistically from stage to the big screen. Following the success of his first two films beginning in 2005, Perry has since written, directed, and produced nineteen stage plays, twenty-four films (with additional ones in production), and eight television shows. He has also produced or executive produced a number of other films, has starred or had a role in numerous non–Tyler Perry films, and is the author of two books.

The most frequently asked question among all of Perry's interviews is how Madea came to exist. Perry shares that Madea came into existence in his third play, *I Can Do Bad All by Myself* in 2000. Mabel Simmons, affectionately known as Madea is a six-foot-five-inch, obese, cantankerous, trash-talking, take-no-mess, marijuana-smoking, gun-toting, antichurch-going grandmother. Although Madea is not the center of any of Tyler Perry's plays, she provides comic relief to complex situations such as domestic abuse, drug addiction, and unstable family structures by misquoting or totally fabricating biblical scriptures. Madea also articulates good old-fashioned mother wit to family and friends. "Mother wit" is a term in African American folklore that refers to the ability to rely on common sense in dealing with life's circumstances. However, in Madea's case, mother wit is usually accompanied by a .38 special and threats of bodily harm. Perry claims that Madea is a combination of the character traits in his mother and aunt. Perry reveals that his playing Madea was born in Chicago. He had hired a well-known singer to play Madea but when she did not show up, he had to don the fat suit and wig to play her. The audience did not seem to mind so he continued. Perry often acknowledges that Madea is widely responsible for his accumulation of the wealth he currently enjoys, and the character has become a brand unto herself.

Although Tyler Perry is praised by many for his comedic characters and spiritual reflections, others criticize him for repetition of storylines and predictable plots. Scholars, social critics, and mere viewers of Perry's films and television shows consistently argue that his images are not progressive nor unique in any way and merely reinforce the media stereotypes that have plagued the African American community for decades. However, in interviews, Perry is always specifically asked about the criticisms from veteran filmmaker Spike Lee. Interviewers recall for Perry how, in a 2009 interview with media host Ed Gordon, Spike Lee compared Perry's portrayal of African Americans in his films to *Amos 'n' Andy*, the first black situation comedy to be broadcast nationally in the 1950s and which contained stereotypical roles of African Americans. Lee said that he does not expect Perry's films to reflect his own vision of black America, but he insists that "imaging" of the African American community is significant. Although Perry has received strong criticisms, he repeatedly tells audiences in interviews that his faithful fan base understands his perspective and supports his products, and, as long as they do, he will continue the work. The relationship between artist and critic is complex, but for Perry the slightest criticism is a personal attack.

Another popular topic of inquiry for Perry and a significant identifier of the Tyler Perry brand is Tyler Perry Studios. It has the distinction of being the first major film studio in the country to be owned exclusively by an African American. Perry's first studio, the 200,000-square-foot facility, located in the abandoned Delta Airlines headquarters in Atlanta, opened in October 2008. In 2010, Perry announced the formation of 34th Street Films, an art-house division of Tyler Perry Studios. 34th Street Films is a studio within Tyler Perry Studios that is for noncomedy films. In 2015, Perry acquired the 330-acre former military base Fort McPherson, located on the southwestern side of Atlanta for $30 million, which he converted to the new Tyler Perry Studios. The HBO Films/OWN production of *The Immortal Life of Henrietta Lacks* and the television series *The Walking Dead* were filmed at the Tyler Perry Studios. Most notable, the Village of Wakanda in the mega-hit movie *Black Panther* was filmed at the studios. Tyler Perry Studios have a replica of a luxury hotel lobby, a 16,000-square-foot mansion, a mock cheap hotel, and a trailer park. It will also host twelve sound stages, employ four hundred people, and have 60,000-square-feet of soundstage. It is reportedly one of the largest studios in the country.

Tyler Perry maintains a very vigorous presence on social media. In addition to his website, www.TylerPerry.com, which provides a listing and synopsis of all of his productions, he also maintains three very popular Facebook accounts. Tyler Perry Facebook site has over thirteen million followers. Tyler Perry Studios Facebook has over eleven million followers, and Madea's Facebook site has five million followers. Perry also communicates regularly on Twitter and shares photos and videos on Instagram.

Most of Perry's radio and television appearances are to promote upcoming Tyler Perry films. Interviewers are curious about the storylines of soon-to-be released movies and what it is like working with whomever the well-known celebrity may be in the current film being promoted. For instance, in the first interview, Perry talks to Tonisha Johnson about Shemar Moore in the role of Orlando in his movie, *Diary of a Mad Black Woman*. By 2012, Hollywood had taken note of Tyler Perry not only as a screenwriter, producer, and director but also as an actor. As such, Perry talks about how it feels to take directions from someone else. In 2012, Perry performed the role of Admiral Richard Barnett in the feature film *Star Trek*. In addition, in 2012, Perry took over the role of Alex Cross (in the titular role). Morgan Freeman had previously played the role. Other roles included *Gone Girl* (2014) in the role of Tanner Bolt; *Brain on Fire*(2016), as Richard; *The Star* (2017), as the voice of Cyrus the Camel; *Backseat* (2018), in the role of Colin Powell. Perry has also been tapped to play Oscar Micheaux for an HBO film (production has not started nor has a title been selected). Micheaux was an African American author, film director, and independent producer of more than forty-four films and was the most successful African American filmmaker of the first half of the twentieth century.

Tyler Perry has come a long way from his days of working odd jobs to survive. He has emerged as one of the most powerful multimedia moguls in the country, part of the Hollywood elite as one of his interviewers calls him. Perry has produced an impressive body of work by rejecting Hollywood's procedures and following his own personal template. For example, Perry owns 100 percent of his films. His productions are finalized much quicker and with a lower budget than the Hollywood approach, and generate significantly higher returns. In one year, Perry directed a hundred episodes of the *House of Payne*. During the same year, he also filmed two movies. Perry can complete a project in thirty days that would take a hundred days to complete in Hollywood. He has built a system that enables him to produce his films and television shows in half the time and often at a fraction of the costs of a typical Hollywood production. He often cites his faith as the driving force behind his survival, creativity, tenacity, and phenomenal success.

This collection of interviews contributes to the growing interest in Tyler Perry. It also serves as a resource for researchers and fans of the filmmaker who will be able to understand Perry better through his own words. *Tyler Perry: Interviews* conform to the standards set by the University Press of Mississippi for its Conversations with Filmmakers Series. This means that the interviews herein appear chronologically and have not been substantially edited from the form of their initial publication or airing. Because of this format, some interviews necessarily repeat information, particularly biographical and introductory information as well as questions and responses in the form of anecdotes and observations. This in itself is useful. Attentive readers will gain an understanding of Perry from noting the consistencies or inconsistencies in his responses to often-asked questions. In some cases, the inconsistency may simply be not remembering previous answers to recurrent questions. However, in other cases, the inconsistency may signal a change in perspective due to his growth as a playwright, filmmaker or television writer, and director.

Tyler Perry has made numerous and major achievements for which he has been widely acknowledged. His accomplishments include creating a successful brand which did not follow the Hollywood formula; building one of the largest movie studios in the country; employing more African Americans in front of and behind the camera than any other studio; creating cinematic content for audiences other filmmakers had ignored; and his philanthropic work. In short, Perry has established himself as a highly successful, thriving auteur responsible for every aspect of a film's presentation. On October 27, 2018, *Forbes* reports that Tyler Perry has sold more than $100 million in tickets, $30 million in his shows, and an estimated $20 million in merchandise, "and that the 300 live shows he produces each year are attended by an average of 35,000 people a week." I have been enlightened and inspired by his journey as have the numerous and diverse media personalities who have had the pleasure of interviewing him. And so, I take pleasure in presenting some of those interviews in this volume, offering Tyler Perry as a worthy subject in this series. I can only hope that readers will also be enlightened and inspired by his journey

Appreciation is extended to all the interviewers and their media outlets whose interviews are included in this volume. I would be remiss if I did not acknowledge my former editor Leila Salisbury, who accepted my proposal to include Tyler Perry in the Conversations with Filmmaker Series. But I am truly grateful to my current editor Craig Gill and his assistant, Emily Bandy, for their assistance and enduring patience in allowing me to complete this volume and for their unwavering support for this project. Thanks to other staff members at the University Press of Mississippi who had a role in the production of this volume. Special thanks to Ashley Palmer, Northern Illinois University, who reviewed earlier drafts of this introduction. Finally, I want to thank my colleague and best friend, Dr. Katherine Grace Hendrix, at the University of Memphis, who has offered me regular doses of encouragement and inspiration in my academic journey since meeting her twenty-five years ago.

JDH

Chronology

1969 Born Emmitt Perry Jr. on September 14 in New Orleans, Louisiana, to Willie Maxine and Emmitt Sr. Perry experiences a strained and abusive childhood at the hands of his father, which leads him to suffer from depression as a teenager.

1985 Perry changes his first name to Tyler to separate himself from his father and start a new life. Drops out of high school but eventually earns a general equivalency diploma.

1990 Perry moves to Atlanta, Georgia, from New Orleans to pursue his dream of directing and starring in one of his plays.

1992 Perry begins his career as a dramatist. Inspired by a comment made by Oprah Winfrey on her talk show, he begins writing letters addressed to himself which later serve as the basis for the play, *I Know I've Been Changed*. The play is staged in Atlanta. Attendance and reviews are very disappointing.

1998 Perry succeeds in reworking and presenting his play, *I Know I've Been Changed*, with a mainstream launch, first at the House of Blues in Atlanta, then at the Fox Theatre. The play begins to be well received with packed houses and good reviews drawing attention from investors.

2000 Perry's play *I Can Do Bad All by Myself* introduces the Madea character. The show is an immediate success and the character proves to be so popular that Perry continues to perform as Madea.

2001 Perry produces *Diary of a Mad Black Woman* followed by *Madea's Family Reunion*. Both receive positive reviews. Perry receives the Helen Hayes Award for Excellence in Theater.

2003 After coming up with *Madea's Class Reunion*, Perry begins touring to promote all his plays. Perry receives the Helen Hayes Award for Excellence in Theater.

2004 Perry is named Black Business Professionals Entrepreneur of the Year.

2005 Perry makes a move to the silver screen February 24 with his film, *Diary of a Mad Black Woman*, which debuts at #1. He receives two BET Comedy Awards: Outstanding Actor in a Theatrical Film and Outstanding Writer of a Theatrical Film, and is also winner of the Black Movie Award for Outstanding Achievement in Writing and the MTV Movie Award for Breakthrough Male for his performance. Perry receives the Stinkers Bad Movie Award in the Worst Supporting Actor category. Perry launches the Tyler Perry website averaging up to 35,000 viewers per week.

2006 *Madea's Family Reunion* is released as a movie February 24, which Perry directs, produces, and stars in. It brings in more than $63 million. Perry establishes his own movie and acting studio in Atlanta, Georgia. Perry's first book, *Don't Make a Black Woman Take Off Her Earrings: Madea's Uninhibited Commentaries on Love and Life*, is released and shoots to the top of the *New York Times* nonfiction bestseller list, remaining there for eight weeks. The book receives the Quill Book Awards for both the Humor and Book of the Year, an unprecedented achievement for a first-time author. Stage plays *What's Done in the Dark*, *Madea Goes to Jail*, and *Why Did I Get Married?* are produced and performed. Perry creates the television comedy series, *House of Payne.*

2007 *Daddy's Little Girls*, a romantic comedy, is released on February 14, grossing over $31 million. *Why Did I Get Married?* is released on Oct. 12. Perry stars in a non-Madea role. *House of Payne*, a family comedy, debuts on TBS on June 6, marking Perry's entry into television programming. Perry is honored at BET's Celebration of Gospel. Playwright Donna West files a lawsuit against Perry and Lionsgate, claiming that Perry stole elements of her play, *Fantasy of a Black Woman*, to create *Diary of a Mad Black Woman.*

2008 West's lawsuit is dismissed. Tyler Perry Studios opens in Atlanta, Georgia. Stage play *The Marriage Counselor* is produced and performed. *Meet the Browns* is released on March 21. On September 12, *The Family that Preys* is released and grosses over $37.1 million. *Essence* and *Time* magazines name Perry one of the most influential people of the year. Perry is named one of *People Magazine*'s 25 Most Intriguing People. He receives three NAACP Awards and the Movieguild Award for Most Inspirational Film for *The Family that Preys*. AARP Movies for Grownup Awards names *The Family that Preys* the Best Buddy Picture Award of the Year. Perry is presented with the Brandon Tartikoff Legacy Award for extraordinary passion, leadership, independence, and vision in the process of creating television programming.

2009 *Madea Goes to Jail* opens on February 20 at #1, grossing $41 million. *I Can Do Bad All by Myself* is released on September 11. The stage play *Laugh to Keep from Crying* is produced and performed. Perry teams up with Oprah Winfrey to present *Precious*, a film based on the novel *Push* by Sapphire (Romana Lofton). On July 20, Perry sponsors sixty-five children from a Philadelphia day camp to visit Walt Disney World after reading that a suburban swim club had shunned them. On December 8, Willie Maxine Perry dies at age sixty-four following an illness. Perry plays Admiral Richard Barnett in *Star Trek*, which opens May 8. Perry receives the BET Honors Media Award. He is named one of *People Magazine*'s Most Intriguing People. *Essence Magazine* lists Perry on their Power List. *Meet the Browns* debuts on TBS January 7. *Madea Goes to Jail* debuts at #1 in the US on February 20. Perry is honored by BET for his accomplishments and receives the Brandon Tartikoff Legacy Award. Perry is sued for copyright infringement by the estate of gospel singer Bertha V. James, who allege James wrote the lyrics for the song, "When I Think of the Goodness of Jesus," in 1950, and allege that Perry incorporated an entire verse of James's work, willfully without permission for *Madea Goes to Jail*. Perry donates $1 million to victims of the earthquakes in Haiti; $110,000 to Covenant House, an organization dedicated to helping homeless youth; and $1 million to the NAACP in celebration of its one hundredth anniversary, reportedly the largest single donation from a private individual to a civil rights organization. Perry is also part of a coalition that comes together to provide Atlanta with $32 million to acquire a set of Martin Luther King Jr.'s working papers.

2010   *Why Did I Get Married Too?*, the sequel to *Why Did I Get Married?*, is released on April 2. Following the critically acclaimed film, *Precious*, Perry announces the formation of 34th Street Films, an arthouse division of Tyler Perry Studios. Perry directs *For Colored Girls*, an adaptation to Ntozake Shange's 1995 choreopoem, *For Colored Girls Who Have Considered Suicide when the Rainbow Is Enuf*. The movie is released on November 5. *For Colored Girls* is named one of the Top 10 Films of the Year by the African American Film Critics Association. The stage play *Madea's Big Happy Family* is produced and performed. Perry receives the Chairman's Award from the NAACP. Lionsgate announces plans to begin releasing Perry's films in the UK. Perry makes *Forbes*'s List of Highest Paid Men in Entertainment and receives the Chairman's Award from the NAACP, four African American Film Critics Association awards, and two NAACP image awards. Perry donates money to rebuild a home for an elderly Georgia woman and her granddaughter when their house burns down. Perry funds the construction of twenty homes for Hurricane Katrina victims, a community named Perry Place in his honor.

2011   Perry's films gross over $500 million worldwide. *Madea's Big Happy Family* is released on April 22. Perry is the recipient of two NAACP Image Awards: Outstanding Motion Picture for *For Colored Girls* and Outstanding Comedy Series for *House of Payne*. He receives MTV Awards for Outstanding

Directing for a Motion Picture/TV Movie and Outstanding Motion Picture for *For Colored Girls*. Perry is the recipient of the Visionary Award from Cinema, USA. He is also the recipient of the Chairman's Award from the National Action Network. Three stage plays are released: *A Madea Christmas*, *Aunt Bam's Place*, and *The Haves and the Have Nots*. Perry's new drama series, *The Haves and the Have Nots*, is the first originally scripted series for OWN, followed by *For Better or For Worse*. Perry executive produces, writes, and directs both series. *Love Thy Neighbor* also debuts on TLC. The series marks the first scripted show for TLC. Perry makes *Forbes*'s List of Highest Paid Men in Entertainment in addition to numerous image awards.

2012   *Madea's Witness Protection* is released on June 29, which grosses over $65 million. On February 24, Perry releases *Good Deeds*. The movie grosses over $30 million. Author Terri Donald alleges *Good Deeds* was based off her book, *Bad Apples Can Be Good Fruit*. The stage play *Madea Gets a Job* is produced and performed. Perry signs exclusive deal with OWN, amounting to the biggest programming deal made since its premiere. Tyler Perry Studios is devastated by a major fire. Less than four months later, a second fire breaks out. Perry stars as the titular character in his first non-Perry movie, *Alex Cross*, the role previously performed by Morgan Freeman. The movie opens on October 19 to critical acclaim and grosses $25,863,915. Perry is awarded an NAACP Image Award for *House of Payne*.

2013   On March 29, Perry releases his thirteenth film, *Temptation: Confessions of a Marriage Counselor*, based on his 2008 play, *The Marriage Counselor*. Perry produces *Tyler Perry Presents Peeples*, which is released on May 1. *A Madea Christmas* is released on December 13. Perry announces that he will release a new film, *Single Mom's Club*, slated to open on May 9, 2014. Perry receives the Pioneer Award from the Black Film Critics Circle. *The Haves and the Have Nots* debuts on OWN on May 28, marking the first scripted series for the network. Perry receives Pioneer Award recipient by the Black Film Critics Circle and two NAACP image awards. Screenwriter William James files a lawsuit claiming that Perry's *Temptation: Confessions of a Marriage Counselor*, was lifted from James's 2009 script *Lovers Kill*.

2014   On February 4 *The Haves and the Have Nots* comes in as the most-watched program on cable television. On March 11 the *Haves and the Have Nots* season two episode sets an OWN record when it scores the highest ratings in the network's history. *Single Mom's Club* opens on March 14. It grosses over $15 million. *If Loving You is Wrong* debuts on OWN on September 9. Perry has a supporting role as Tanner Bolt in the thriller, *Gone Girl*, which opens October 3. Stage play, *Madea's Hell Hath No Fury Like a Woman Scorned* is produced and performed. Perry and girlfriend Gelila Bekele celebrate the birth of a baby boy, Aman. Perry receives the Golden Raspberry Award in the worst actress category for *A Madea Christmas*. Perry is the recipient of the Jackie Robinson Foundation Honors and *Essence*'s Black Men in Hollywood Honors. Perry receives the Directors Guild of America Honors and African American Film Critics Association Award for Best Supporting Actor in *Gone Girl*, and makes *Forbes*'s Celebrity 100 List (#56).

2015   Perry's first animated movie, *Madea's Tough Love*, is released for DVD distribution. Perry purchases the former Fort McPherson Army Base for $30 million to be the new home of Tyler Perry Studios. Perry receives the Gracie Award for *The Haves and the Have Nots* from the Directors Guild of America.

2016   *Boo! A Madea Halloween* is Perry's seventeenth film and the ninth film within the Madea franchise. It opens on October 21. Perry, along with J. J. Abrams and Steven Spielberg, becomes a member of the Atom Tickets Advisory Board, a movie ticket start-up company. Perry is the narrator in *The Passion*, a television movie on the life of Jesus which airs in March. On May 7 Perry delivers the commencement address at Tuskegee University and is given an honorary doctorate degree. Perry plays Baxter Stockman in *Teenage Mutant Ninja Turtles: Out of the Shadows*, which opens June 3. *Too Close to Home* debuts on TLC on August 22. Perry makes the *Hollywood Reporter*'s List of the 100 Most Powerful People in Hollywood (#71).

2017   Perry lands a film-and-TV-production deal with Viacom, agreeing to produce ninety episodes annually of original drama and comedy series for BET and Viacom networks. The film deal starts immediately but the TV and video component will begin in 2019 when his contract with OWN expires. The Viacom deal will run through 2024. Perry is featured on *Oprah's Master Class* on OWN on August 3, where he discusses his successes, failures, and motivations. Perry receives the People's Choice Humanitarian Award in recognition of his efforts to change lives all over the world for the better. Perry makes *Forbes*'s rich list. Perry receives the Morehouse College Award—Three Candles in the Dark Honors. The stage play *Madea on the Run* is produced and performed. On November 17, Columbia Pictures releases *The Star*, an animation movie in which Perry plays the character Cyrus. *Brain on Fire* is released by Netflix on February 22; Perry plays the character Richard. A Detroit-based entertainment company claims that Perry took the plot of one of its plays and used it for his hit show, *The Haves and the Have Nots*. The lawsuit claims that the plot is significantly like the plot of *Affairs*, a script and play created by playwright Vanessa Lynn. *Affairs* debuted in 2008. Perry's second book, *Higher Is Waiting* is released in November and is #5 on the *New York Times* best-seller list.

2018   *The Paynes*, a spin-off of *The House of Payne*, debuts January 9 on OWN. *Acrimony* (previously titled *She's Living My Life*) debuts March 30. Perry plays former US Joint Chief of Staff, Colin Powell in *Vice* (previously titled *Backseat*), a biopic on former Vice President Dick Cheney. Author Terri Donald alleges *Good Deeds* was based off her book, *Bad Apples Can Be Good Fruit;* Donald claims that she sent a copy to Perry well before his film was made and sought $225,000 in damages as well as an injunction to add a book credit in the opening and closing credits. Perry receives the Razzie Award for Worst Actress in *BOO 2! A Madea Halloween*.

2019   *A Madea Family Funeral* (previously titled *A Family Funeral*) to be released this year. Perry is slated to depict Oscar Michauex, who was the first black filmmaker in America, in an HBO original movie. Perry teams with CJ E&M, Korea's largest entertainment conglomerate, to produce an English-language remake of the Korean hit film, *Miss Granny*. The production will be targeted at the African American community.

Filmography

DIARY OF A MAD BLACK WOMAN (2005)
Tyler Perry Studios
Distributor: Lionsgate Films
Producers: **Tyler Perry** and Reuben Cannon
Executive Producers: Michael Poseornek, John Dellaverson, Robert L. Johnson, and **Tyler Perry**
Director: Darren Grant
Screenwriter: **Tyler Perry**
Genres: Comedy, Drama, Romance
Director of Cinematography: David Claessen
Production Designer: Ina Mayhew
Film Editor: Terilyn A. Shropshire
Music Editor: Elvin D. Ross
Casting Directors: Shay Griffin and Kim Williams
Cast: Kimberly Elise, Steve Harris, Shemar Moore, Tamara Taylor, Lisa Marcos, Tiffany Evans, Cicely Tyson, **Tyler Perry**, Tamela Mann, Mablean Ephriam
Synopsis: A couple's seemingly happy marriage crumbles when the wife discovers that her husband has another family and intends to divorce her to be with them.
Run Time: 1hr 43min
Box Office: $72,513,600

MADEA'S FAMILY REUNION (2006)
Tyler Perry Studios
Distributor: Lionsgate Films
Producers: Reuben Cannon and Mike Upton
Executive Producers: Michael Paseornek and **Tyler Perry**
Director: **Tyler Perry**
Screenwriter: **Tyler Perry**
Genres: Comedy, Drama, Romance
Director of Cinematography: Toyomichi Kurita
Production Designer: Ina Mayhew

Film Editor: John Carter
Music Editors: **Tyler Perry** and Elvin Ross
Casting Editors: Shay Griffin and Kim Williams
Cast: **Tyler Perry**, Blair Underwood, Lynn Whitfield, Boris Kodjoe, Henry
Simmons, Lisa Arrindell Anderson, Rochelle Aytes, Tangi Miller, Keke Palmer,
Cicely Tyson, Maya Angelou, Cassi Davis, Johnny Gill, Mablean Ephriam,
Nicholas Ortiz
Synopsis: While planning her family's reunion, Madea must also contend with
her love-troubled nieces and be a court-ordered foster mother to a runaway teen.
Run Time: 1hr 49min
Box Office: $88,657,700

WHY DID I GET MARRIED? (2007)
Tyler Perry Studios
Distributor: Lionsgate Films
Producers: Reuben Cannon and **Tyler Perry**
Executive Producer: Michael Paseornek
Director: **Tyler Perry**
Screenwriter: **Tyler Perry**
Genres: Comedy, Drama
Director of Cinematography: Toyomichi Kurita
Production Designer: Ina Mayhew
Film Editor: Maysie Hoy
Music Editor: Aaron Zigman
Casting Director: Alpha Tyler
Cast: **Tyler Perry**, Janet Jackson, Jill Scott, Malik Yoba, Richard T. Jones,
Michael Jai White, Denise Boutte, Lamman Rucker, Sharon Leal, Tasha Smith,
Keesha Sharp
Synopsis: The screen adaptation of Perry's stage play about the trials of marriage
as it effects four couples.
Run Time: 1hr 58min
Box Office: $73,659,500

DADDY'S LITTLE GIRLS (2007)
Tyler Perry Studios
Distributor: Lionsgate Films
Producers: **Tyler Perry** and Reuben Cannon
Executive Producer: Michael Paseornek
Director: **Tyler Perry**
Screenwriter: **Tyler Perry**

Genres: Drama, Romance
Director of Cinematography: Toyomichi Kurita
Production Designer: Ina Mayhew
Film Editor: Maysie Hoy, A.C.E.
Music Editor: Brian McKnight
Casting Directors: Shay Griffin and Kim Williams
Cast: Gabrielle Union, Idris Elba, Louis Gossett Jr., Tasha Smith, Tracee Ellis
Ross, Malinda Williams, Terri J. Vaughn, Gary Sturgis, Cassi Davis, LaVan Davis,
China McClain, Lauryn Alisa McClain, Sierra McClain, Craig Robinson, Timon
Kyle Durrett
Synopsis: A mechanic enlists the help of an arrogant, successful, but lonely attorney while trying to gain custody of his three daughters from his treacherous
exwife and her drug-dealing boyfriend.
Run Time: 1hr 40min
Box Office: $41,853,000

THE FAMILY THAT PREYS (2008)
Tyler Perry Studios
Distributor: Lionsgate Films
Producers: Reuben Cannon, **Tyler Perry**, Joseph P. Genier, and Roger M. Bobb
Executive Producer: Michael Paseornek
Director: **Tyler Perry**
Screenwriter: **Tyler Perry**
Genre: Drama
Director of Cinematography: Toyomichi Kurita
Production Designer: Ina Mayhew
Film Editor: Maysie Hoy
Music Editor: Aaron Zigman
Casting Director: Alpha Tyler
Cast: Kathy Bates, Alfre Woodard, Sanaa Lathan, **Tyler Perry**, Rockmond
Dunbar, Taraji P. Henson, KaDee Strickland, Cole Hauser, Robin Givens
Synopsis: Two families' lives—one wealthy, the other working class—are intertwined in both business and love.
Run Time: 1hr 51min
Box Office: $47,441,000

MEET THE BROWNS (2008)
Tyler Perry Studios
Distributor: Lionsgate Films
Producers: Reuben Cannon and **Tyler Perry**

Executive Producer: Michael Paseornek
Director: **Tyler Perry**
Screenwriter: **Tyler Perry**
Genres: Comedy, Drama, Romance
Director of Cinematography: Sandi Sissel, ASC
Production Designer: Ina Mayhew
Film Editor: Maysie Hoy
Music Editor: Aaron Zigman
Casting Director: Kim Williams
Cast: Angela Bassett, Rick Fox, Margaret Avery, Frankie Faison, Jenifer Lewis, Lance Gross, David Mann, Tamela Mann, Irma P. Hall, LaVan Davis, Phillip Van Lear, **Tyler Perry**
Synopsis: A struggling single mom takes her children to Georgia for the funeral of her father—a man she never met. There, her family is introduced to the crass but loving Brown family.
Run time: 1hr 41min
Box Office: $53,667,700

I CAN DO BAD ALL BY MYSELF (2009)
Tyler Perry Studios
Distributor: Lionsgate Films
Producers: Reuben Cannon and **Tyler Perry**
Executive Producer: Michael Paseornek
Director: **Tyler Perry**
Screenwriter: **Tyler Perry**
Genres: Comedy, Drama
Director of Cinematography: Alexander Gruszynski
Production Designer: Ina Mayhew
Film Editor: Maysie Hoy, A.C.E.
Music Editor: Aaron Zigman
Casting Director: Alpha Tyler
Cast: Taraji P. Henson, Adam Rodriquez, **Tyler Perry**, Hope Olaide Wilson, Brian J. White, Gladys Knight, Frederick Siglar, Kwesi Boakye, Mary J. Blige, Marvin Winans
Synopsis: When Madea catches a teenage girl and her younger brothers looting her home, she takes matters into her own hands and delivers the young delinquents to the only relative they have—their aunt April, a heavy-drinking nightclub singer.
Run Time: 1hr 53min
Box Office: $51,733,921

MADEA GOES TO JAIL (2009)
Tyler Perry Studios
Distributor: Lionsgate Films
Producers: Reuben Cannon and **Tyler Perry**
Executive Producer: Michael Paseornek
Director: **Tyler Perry**
Screenplay: **Tyler Perry**
Genres: Comedy, Crime, Drama
Director of Cinematography: Alexander Gruszynaki
Production Designer: Ina Mayhew
Film Editor: Maysie Hoy
Music Editor: Aaron Zigman
Casting Director: Kimberly Hardin
Cast: **Tyler Perry**, Keisha Knight Pulliam, Derek Luke, Tamela Mann, Robin
Coleman, Benjamin Benítez, Sofía Vergara, David Mann, Viola Davis, Ion
Overman, RonReaco Lee, Vanessa Ferlito
Synopsis: Following a high-speed freeway chase, Madea is arrested and lands in
jail where she meets a variety of mixed-up characters.
Run Time: 1hr 42min
Box Office: $115,719,600

PRECIOUS (2009)
Based on the novel *Push* by Sapphire
Distributor: Lionsgate Films
Producers: Roger M. Bobb, Paul Hall, and **Tyler Perry**
Executive Producers: Joseph P. Genier Michael Paseornek, Nzingha Stewart,
Tyler Perry, and Oprah Winfrey
Director: Lee Daniels
Screenwriter: Geoffrey Fletcher (based on the novel *Push* by Sapphire)
Genre: Drama
Director of Cinematography: Andrew Dunn
Production Designer: Roshelle Berliner
Film Editor: Joe Klotz
Music Editor: Mario Grigorov
Film Editor: Joe Klotz
Casting Directors: Billy Hopkins and Jessica Kelly
Cast: Mo'Nique, Paula Patton, Mariah Carey, Sherri Shepherd, Lenny Kravitz,
Gabourey Sidibe
Synopsis: An overweight, abused, and illiterate teen who is pregnant with her

second child by her father is invited to enroll in an alternative school in hopes that her life can head in a new direction.
Run Time: 2hr 13min
Box Office: $63.6M

FOR COLORED GIRLS (2010)
Tyler Perry Studios
Distributed by: Lionsgate Films
Producers: **Tyler Perry**, Roger M. Bobb, and Paul Hall
Executive Producers: Ozzie Areu, Joseph P. Genier, Nzingha Stewart, and Michael Paseornek
Director: **Tyler Perry**
Screenwriter: **Tyler Perry** (based on the stage play *For Colored Girls Who Have Considered Suicide When the Rainbow Is Enuf*, written by Ntozake Shange)
Genre: Drama
Director of Cinematography: Alexander Gruszynski, ASC
Production Designer: Ina Mayhew
Film Editor: Maysie Hoy, A.C.E.
Music Editor: Aaron Zigman
Casting Director: Robi Reed
Cast: Kimberly Elise, Janet Jackson, Michael Ealy, Loretta Devine, Thandie Newton, Phylicia Rashad, Omari Hardwick, Hill Harper, Aniki Noni Rose, Tessa Thompson, Whoopi Goldberg, Kerry Washington, Macy Gray, Khalil Kain, Richard Lawson
Synopsis: Nine women's lives are intertwined as each one deals with issues that impact all women in general and women of color in particular. Each woman portrays one of the characters in Ntozake Shange's 1995 choreopoem, "For Colored Girls Who Have Considered Suicide/When the Rainbow Is Enuf."
Run Time: 2hr 14min
Box Office: $38M

WHY DID I GET MARRIED TOO? (2010)
Tyler Perry Studios
Distributor: Lionsgate Films
Producers: **Tyler Perry** and Reuben Cannon
Executive Producer: Michael Paseornek
Director: **Tyler Perry**
Screenwriter: **Tyler Perry**
Genres: Comedy, Drama
Director of Cinematography: Toyomichi Kurita

Production Designer: Ina Mayhew
Film Editor: Maysie Hoy, A.C.E.
Music Editor: Aaron Zigman
Casting Director: Alpha Tyler
Cast: **Tyler Perry**, Janet Jackson, Tasha Smith, Jill Scott, Sharon Leal, Malik Yoba, Lamman Rucker, Michael Jai White, Louis Gossett Jr., Cicely Tyson
Synopsis: Four couples find themselves struggling to save their marriages once again on their annual marriage retreat, while each of them battle through various issues.
Run Time: 2hr 0min
Box Office: $60.1M

MADEA'S BIG HAPPY FAMILY (2011)
Tyler Perry Studios
Distributed by: Lionsgate Films
Producers: **Tyler Perry**, Rueben Cannon, and Roger M. Bobb
Executive Producers: Ozzie Areu, Joseph P. Genier, and Michael Paseornek
Director: **Tyler Perry**
Screenwriter: **Tyler Perry**
Genres: Comedy, Drama
Director of Cinematography: Toyomichi Kurita
Production Designer: Ina Mayhew
Film Editor: Maysie Hoy, A.C.E.
Music Editor: Aaron Zigman
Casting Director: Kim Williams
Cast: Isaiah Mustafa, Loretta Devine, Shad "Bow Wow" Gregory Moss, **Tyler Perry**, Cassi Davis, Rodney Perry, Teyana Taylor, Natalie Desselle, Phillip Anthony-Rodriquez, Maury Povitch
Synopsis: Madea tries to bring her squabbling family together for a family dinner on behalf of her niece who needs to discuss her health with them.
Run Time: 1hr 46min
Box Office: $54M

MADEA'S WITNESS PROTECTION (2012)
Tyler Perry Studios
Distributor: Lionsgate Films
Producers: **Tyler Perry**, Ozzie Areu, and Paul Hall
Executive Producer: John J. Kelly and Michael Paseornek
Director: **Tyler Perry**
Screenwriter: **Tyler Perry**

Genre: Comedy
Director of Cinematography: Alexander Gruszynski
Production Designer: Eloise C. Stammerjohn
Film Editor: Maysie Hoy
Music Editor: Aaron Zigman
Casting Director: Kim Coleman
Cast: **Tyler Perry**, Eugene Levy, Denise Richards, Romeo Miller, Doris Roberts, Tom Arnold, John Amos, Marla Gibbs, Danielle Campbell, Devan Leos
Synopsis: A Wall Street investment banker has been set up as the linchpin of his company's mob-backed Ponzi scheme and is relocated with his family to Madea's southern home.
Run Time: 1hr 54min
Box Office: $67M

GOOD DEEDS (2012)
Tyler Perry Studios
Distributor: Lionsgate Films
Producers: **Tyler Perry**, Paul Hall, and Ozzie Areu
Executive Producer: Michael Paseornek
Director: **Tyler Perry**
Screenplay: **Tyler Perry**
Genres: Comedy, Romance
Director of Photography: Alexander Gruszynski
Production Designer: Ira Mayhew
Film Editor: Maysie Hoy
Music Editor: Aaron Zigman
Casting Director: Kim Coleman
Cast: Rebecca Romijn, Thandie Newton, **Tyler Perry**, Gabrielle Union, Jamie Kennedy, Eddie Cibrian, Brian White, Phylicia Rashad, Beverly Johnson, Jordenn Thompson
Synopsis: Businessman Wesley Deeds is jolted out of his scripted life when he meets Lindsey, a struggling single mother who is a cleaning woman in his office building.
Run Time: 1hr 51min
Box Office: $35.6 M

A MADEA CHRISTMAS (2013)
Tyler Perry Studios
Distributor: Lionsgate Films
Producers: **Tyler Perry**, Ozzie Areu, Matt Moore, and Jennifer Booth

Executive Producer: Michael Paseornek
Director: **Tyler Perry**
Screenwriter: **Tyler Perry**
Genres: Drama, Comedy
Director of Cinematography: Alexander Grunzynski
Production Designer: Eloise C. Stammerjohn
Film Editor: Maysie Hoy
Music Editor: Christopher Young
Casting Directors: Kim Coleman and Rhavynn Drummer
Cast**: Tyler Perry**, Chad Michael Murray, Larry the Cable Guy, Alicia Witt, Kathy Najimy, Eric Lively, Lisa Whelchel, Tika Sumpter
Synopsis: Madea shares her unique form of holiday cheer in a rural town when she is coaxed into helping a friend pay her daughter a surprise visit for Christmas.
Run Time: 1hr 40min
Box Office: $53.4M

PEEPLES (2013)
Tyler Perry Studios
Distributor: Lionsgate Films
Producers: **Tyler Perry**, Stephanie Allan, Ozzie Areu, Paul Hall, Preston L. Holmes, Matt Moore, and H. H. Cooper
Executive Producers: Charles S. Dutton, Preston L. Holmes, Sherry Marsh, and Michael Paseornek
Director: Tina Gordon Chism
Screenwriter: Tina Gordon Chism
Genre: Comedy
Director of Cinematography: Alexander Gruszynski
Production Designer: Eloise C. Stammerjohn
Film Editor: David Moritz
Music Editor: Aaron Zigman
Casting Director: Kim Coleman
Cast: Kerry Washington, Ana Gasteyer, Tyler James Williams, Craig Robinson, Kali Hawk, S. Epatha Merkerson, David Alan Grier, Diahann Carroll, Malcolm Barrett, Melvin Van Peebles
Synopsis: Sparks fly when Wade Walker crashes the Peeples's family reunion in the Hamptons to ask for daughter Grace's hand in marriage.
Run Time: 1hr 35min
Box Office: $9.3 M

TEMPTATION: CONFESSIONS OF A MARRIAGE COUNSELOR (2013)
Tyler Perry Studios
Distributor: Lionsgate Films
Producers: **Tyler Perry**, Ozzie Areu, and Paul Hall
Executive Producers: Michael Paseornek and Michael Upton
Director: **Tyler Perry**
Producers: **Tyler Perry**, Ozzie Areu, and Paul Hall
Screenwriter: **Tyler Perry**
Genre: Drama
Director of Cinematography: Alexander Gruszynski
Production Designer: Eloise C. Stammerjohn
Film Editor: Maysie Hoy
Music Editor: Aaron Zigman
Casting Director: Kim Coleman
Cast: Jurnee Smollett-Bell, Vanessa Williams, Brandy Norwood, Kim
Kardashian, Robbie Jones, Ella Joyce, Jerry Stiller, Lance Gross, Renée Taylor
Synopsis: An ambitious married woman's temptation by a handsome social
media billionaire leads to betrayal and recklessness and forever alters the course
of her life.
Run Time: 1hr 51min
Box Office: $53.1M

SINGLE MOM'S CLUB (2014)
Tyler Perry Studios
Distributor: Lionsgate Films
Producers: **Tyler Perry**, Ozzie Areu, and Matt Moore
Executive Producer: Michael Paseornek
Director: **Tyler Perry**
Screenwriter: **Tyler Perry**
Genres: Drama, Comedy
Director of Cinematography: Alexander Gruszynski
Production Design: Eloise C. Stammerjohn
Film Editor: Maysie Hoy
Music Editor: Christopher Young
Casting Directors: Kim Coleman and Rhavynn Drummer
Cast: **Tyler Perry**, Eddie Cibrian, Amy Smart, Terry Crews, Nia Long, William
Levy, Zulay Henao, Wendi McLendon-Covey, Cocoa Brown, Ryan Eggold
Synopsis: Five struggling single moms put aside their differences to form a sup-
port group.
Run time: 1hr 50min
Box office: $15,973,881

BOO! A MADEA HALLOWEEN (2016)
Tyler Perry Studios
Distributor: Lionsgate Films
Producers: **Tyler Perry**, Ozzie Areu, and Will Areu
Executive Producer: Qiuyun Long
Director: **Tyler Perry**
Screenwriters: **Tyler Perry**; story by Ben Chambers
Genres: Drama, Comedy, Horror
Director of Cinematography: Richard J. Vialet
Production Designer: Crystal Hayslett
Film Editor: Larry Sexton
Music Editor: Elvin Ross
Casting Director: Kim Coleman
Cast: **Tyler Perry**, Cassi Davis, Patrice Lovely, Bella Thorne, Yousef Erakat, Lexy
Panterra, Andre Hall, Brock O'Hurn, Liza Koshy, Diamond White
Synopsis: Madea winds up in the middle of mayhem when she spends Halloween
fending off killers, paranormal poltergeists, ghosts, and ghouls while keeping a
watchful eye on a group of misbehaving teens.
Run time: 1hr 43min
Box office: $73,206,343

BOO 2! A MADEA HALLOWEEN (2017)
Tyler Perry Studios
Distributor: Lionsgate Films
Producers: **Tyler Perry**, Ozzie Areu, Will Areu, and Mark E. Swinton
Executive Producer: **Tyler Perry**
Director: **Tyler Perry**
Screenwriter: **Tyler Perry**
Genres: Drama, Comedy, Horror
Director of Cinematography: Richard J. Vialet
Production Designer: Tom Munroe
Film Editor: Larry Sexton
Music Editor: Philip White
Casting Director: Kim Coleman
Cast: **Tyler Perry**, Lexy Panterra, Diamond White, Brock O'Hurn, Patrice
Lovely, Yousef Erakat, Inanna Sarkis, Cassi Davis
Synopsis: Madea, Bam, and Hattie venture to a haunted campground, and they
must run for their lives when monsters, goblins, and the bogeyman come.
Run Time: 1hr 41min
Box office: $46,649,659

MADEA'S TOUGH LOVE (animated) (2017)
Tyler Perry Studios, Bento Box Entertainment
Distributor: Lionsgate Home Entertainment (DVD)
Producers: **Tyler Perry**, Ozzie Areu, Matt Moore, Eric S. Rollman, and Ken
Katsumoto
Executive Producers: Scott D. Greenburg, Daniel Engelhardt, Joel Kuwahara,
and Mark McJimsey
Animation Producer: Kenny Micka
Director: Frank Marino
Screenwriters: Matt Fleckenstein and Ben Gluck
Genre: Comedy
Director of Cinematography: Timothy Barnes
Production Designer: Sidney Clifton
Film Editor: Larry Sexton
Music Editor: Frank Ciampi
Casting Director: Sidney Clifton
Cast: Voices of **Tyler Perry**, Cassi Davis, Rolanda Watts, Avery Kidd Waddell,
Philip Anthony-Rodriquez, Georg Stanford Brown, Kevin Michael Richardson,
Mari Williams, Indigo, Caitlyn Taylor Love, Maya Kay, Bootsy Collins
Synopsis: After a hilarious run-in with the law, Madea is sentenced to com-
munity service. Determined to do good, she enlists the help of her brother Joe,
Aunt Bam, and the local kids to save the Moms Mabley Youth Center from being
shut down.
Run time: 1hr 4min

NOBODY'S FOOL (2018)
Tyler Perry Studios
Distributor: Paramount Players
Producers: Will Areu and Mark E. Swinton
Director: **Tyler Perry**
Screenwriter: **Tyler Perry**
Genre: Comedy
Director of Cinematography: Richard J. Vialet
Production Designer: Paul Wonsek
Film Editor: Larry Sexton
Music Editor: Johnny Caruso
Casting Director: Kim Coleman
Cast: Tiffany Haddish, Taraji P. Henson, Tika Sumpter, Omari Hardwick, Whoopi
Goldberg, Amber Riley, Missi Pyle, Courtney Henggeler, Frank David Monroe,
Leslie Sides, Trinity Whiteside, Apollo GT

Synopsis: The film follows a woman who gets released from prison and reunites with her sister who is forced to accept that she might be getting catfished by an online boyfriend.

Run time: 1hr 50min

Box Office: $31,713,110

ACRIMONY (2018)

Tyler Perry Studios

Distributor: Lionsgate Films

Producers: **Tyler Perry**, Ozzie Areu, Will Areu, and Mark E. Swinton

Executive Producer: **Tyler Perry**

Director: **Tyler Perry**

Screenwriter: **Tyler Perry**

Genre: Drama

Director of Cinematography: Richard J. Vialet

Production Designer: Patrick Sheedy

Film Editor: Larry Sexton

Music Editor: Johnny Caruso

Casting Directors: Kim Coleman and Rhavynn Drummer

Cast: Jazmyn Simon, Taraji P. Henson, Danielle Nicolet, Tika Sumpter, Ajiona Alexus, Lyriq Bent, Tiffany Sander McKenzie, Tammie Marie Vaughan, Terayle Hill, Shavon Kirksey, Jason Vail, Kendrick Cross, Jay Hunter, Racquel Bianca John, Nelson Estevez, Antonio Madison

Synopsis: A faithful wife becomes enraged when it becomes clear that she has been betrayed by her husband.

Run time: 2hr 0min

Box Office: $43,549,096

A MADEA FAMILY FUNERAL (2019)

Tyler Perry Studios

Distributor: Lionsgate Films

Producer: Ozzie Areu

Executive Producer: **Tyler Perry**

Director: **Tyler Perry**

Screenwriter: **Tyler Perry**

Genre: Comedy

Director of Cinematography: Richard J. Vialet

Production Designer: Patrick Sheedy

Film Editor: Larry Sexton

Music Editor: Johnny Caruso

Casting Directors: Kim Coleman and Rhavynn Drummer
Cast: **Tyler Perry**, Patrice Lovely, Cassi Davis, Ciera Payton, Khaneshia Smith, David Otunga, Quin Walters, Selena Anduze, Chandra Currelley-Young, Vermyttya Erahn, Ary Katz
Synopsis: A family reunion becomes a nightmare when Madea and family travel to rural Georgia, where they find themselves unexpectedly planning a funeral that might also unveil some unsavory family secrets.
Run time: 1hr 42mins
Box Office: $72,385,430

Acting Roles (non–Tyler Perry movies)

STAR TREK (2009)
Genre: Sci-Fi, Action, Adventure
Director: J. J. Abrams
Producers: J. J. Abrams and Damon Lindelof
Screenwriters: Roberto Orci and Alex Kurtzman
Cast: Chris Pine, Zachary Quinto, Eric Bana, Simon Pegg, Winona Ryder, John Cho, Ben Cross, Bruce Greenwood, Zoe Saldana, Karl Urban, Anton Yelchin, Leonard Nimoy, **Tyler Perry**, Jimmy Bennett, Clifton Collins Jr., Marlene Forte, Chris Hemsworth
Synopsis: The story of a young crew's maiden voyage onboard the most advanced starship ever created: the USS *Enterprise*. Amid an incredible journey full of optimism, intrigue, comedy, and cosmic peril, the new recruits must find a way to stop an evil being whose mission of vengeance threatens all of mankind.
Run time: 2hr 7min
Box office: $385,700,000

ALEX CROSS (2012)
Genre: Action, Thriller, Drama
Director: Rob Cohen
Producers: Bill Block, Paul Hanson, Steve Bowen, Leopoldo Gout, Randall Emmett, and James Patterson
Screenwriter: Kerry Williamson and Marc Moss
Cast: **Tyler Perry**, Matthew Fox, Edward Burns, Jean Reno, Rachel Nichols, Giancarlo Esposito, John C. McGinley, Cicely Tyson, Chad Lindberg, Carmen Ejogo
Synopsis: Homicide detective/psychologist Alex Cross face off in a high-stakes game of cat-and-mouse, but when the mission gets personal, Cross is pushed to the edge of his moral and psychological limits in this taut and exciting action thriller.

Run time: 1hr 41min
Box office: $34,600,000

GONE GIRL (2014)
Genre: Drama, Thriller
Director: David Fincher
Producers: David Fincher and Reese Witherspoon
Screenwriters: Gillian Flynn and David Fincher
Cast: Ben Affleck, Rosamund Pike, **Tyler Perry**, Neil Patrick Harris, Kim
Dickens, Patrick Fugit, Missi Pyle, Carrie Coon, Sela Ward, Boyd Holbrook,
Emily Ratajkowski, David Clennon
Synopsis: Based on the global bestseller by Gillian Flynn, *Gone Girl* unearths the
secrets at the heart of a modern marriage. With his wife's disappearance having
become the focus of an intense media circus, a man sees the spotlight on him
when it's suspected that he may not be innocent.
Run time: 2hr 29min
Box office: $369,300,000

THE PASSION (TV) (2016)
Genre: Musical Drama
Directors: David Grifhorst and Robert Deaton
Producers: Allen Shapiro, Mike Mahan, Mark Bracco, Jacco Doornbos, Adam
Anders, and David Grifhorst
Screenwriter: Peter Barsocchini
Cast: Jencarlos Canela, Trisha Yearwood, **Tyler Perry** (narrator), Chris
Daughtry, Seal, Prince Royce, Michael W. Smith, Shane Harper, Yolanda Adams
Synopsis: Set in modern day, *The Passion* follows the dramatic and inspira-
tional story of Jesus of Nazareth as he presides over the Last Supper and then
is betrayed by Judas, put on trial by Pontius Pilate, convicted, crucified, and
resurrected.
Run time: 2hr 0min

TEENAGE MUTANT NINJA TURTLES: OUT OF THE SHADOWS (2016)
Genre: Action, Fantasy
Director: David Green
Producers: Michael Bay, Andrew Form, and Bradley Fuller
Screenwriters: Josh Appelbaum and Andre Nemec
Cast: Stephen Amell, Megan Fox, **Tyler Perry**, Laura Linney, Will Arnett, Tony
Shalhoub, Alessandra Ambrosio, Alan Ritchson, Brian Tee, Danny Woodburn,

Tohoru Masamune, Noel Fisher, Brittany Ishibashi, Jeremy Howard, Fred Armisen

Synopsis: Michelangelo, Donatello, Leonardo, and Raphael return to battle along with a new group of villains and allies.

Run time: 1hr 52min

Box office: $245,600,000

THE STAR (2017)

Columbia Pictures

Genre: Animation, Adventure, Family

Director: Timothy Reckart

Screenwriter: Carlos Kotkin

Cast: Steven Yeun, Gina Rodriquez, Oprah Winfrey, Christopher Plummer, **Tyler Perry,** Tracy Morgan, Kris Kristofferson, Kristin Chenoweth, Kelly Clarkson, Gabriel Iglesias, Ving Rhames, Aidy Bryant

Synopsis: One day a brave donkey named Bo finds the courage to break free and finally go on the adventure of his dreams. On his journey, he teams up with Ruth, a lovable sheep who has lost her flock, and Dave, a dove with lofty aspirations. Along with three wisecracking camels and some eccentric stable animals, Bo and his new friends follow the Star and become accidental heroes in the greatest story ever told—the first Christmas.

Run time: 1hr 26min

Box office: $62,800,000

BRAIN ON FIRE (2017)

Denver and Delilah Productions

Distributor: Netflix

Genres: Biography, Drama

Director: Gerard Barrett

Producers: Charlize Theron, Beth Kono, and A. J. Dix

Screenwriter: Gerard Barrett

Cast: Chloë Grace Moretz, Carrie-Anne Moss, Richard Armitage, **Tyler Perry**, Thomas Mann, Jenny Slate, Nicole LaPlaca, Agam Darshi, Vincent Gale, Navid Negahban

Synopsis: A *New York Post* reporter suffering from a rare autoimmune disorder is repeatedly misdiagnosed following a series of violent outbursts and severe amnesia. Based on Susannah Cahalan's bestselling memoir, *Brain on Fire: My Month of Madness*.

Run time: 1hr 28min

Box office: $19,365

VICE (2018)
Annapurna Pictures
Genres: Biography, Drama
Director: Adam McKay
Screenwriter: Adam McKay
Producers: Will Ferrell, Dede Gardner, Brad Pitt, Adam McKay, and Jeremy Kleiner
Executive Producer: Megan Ellison
Casting Director: Francine Maisler
Cast: Amy Adams, Christian Bale, Sam Rockwell, Bill Pullman, Steve Carell, Alison Pill, Stefania LaVie Owen, Shea Whigham, Lily Rabe, **Tyler Perry**
Synopsis: The story of Dick Cheney, one of the most powerful vice presidents in history, and how his policies changed the world as we know it.
Run time: 2hr 12min
Box office: $47,806,224

OSCAR MICHEAUX (2018)
Sony Pictures (HBO)
Genre: Drama
Director: **TBA**
Screenwriter: Charles Murray
Executive Producers: **Tyler Perry**, Craig Zadan, and Neil Meron
Cast: **Tyler Perry** (other cast members to be announced)
Synopsis: A biopic on the life and career of the pioneering black filmmaker, based on the 2007 biography, *Oscar Micheaux: The Great and Only: The Life of America's First Black Filmmaker* by Patrick McGilligan.

Television Shows

HOUSE OF PAYNE (2007–2012)
Networks: ABC, TBS, and OWN
Genres: Comedy, Drama, Family
Executive Producers: **Tyler Perry**, Ozzie Areu, and Rueben Cannon
Producer: Mark E. Swinton
Directors: **Tyler Perry**, Chip Fields, Kim Fields, and Roger M. Bobb
Cast: Allen Payne, Larramie Doc Shaw, LaVan Davis, Cassi Davis, Denise Burse, China Ann McClain, Demetria McKinney, Lance Gross, Keshia Knight Pulliam
Synopsis: A situation comedy that revolves around the triumphs and struggles of a multi-generational family trying to live together under one roof.

MEET THE BROWNS (2009–2012)
Networks: BET and TBS
Genre: Comedy
Executive Producers: **Tyler Perry** and Roger M. Bobb
Producers: Ozzie Areu, Angi Bones, and Will Areu
Directors: **Tyler Perry**, Kim Fields, Roger M. Bobb, Mark E. Swinton, and
Leonard R. Garner Jr.
Cast: David Mann, Tamela Mann, Lamman Rucker, Denise Boutte, Toney
Vaughn, Juanita Jennings, Gunnar Washington, K. Callan, Jeannette Sousa,
Arielle Vanderberg, Antonio Jamarillo, Logan Browning
Synopsis: In the spinoff from *House of Payne*, Leroy Brown tries to fulfill his
father's dying wish by transforming a dilapidated house into a retirement home.

FOR BETTER OR WORSE (2011–2016)
Networks: OWN and TBS
Genres: Comedy, Drama
Executive Producers: **Tyler Perry** and Ozzie Areu
Producers: Mark E. Swinton and Will Areu
Director: **Tyler Perry**
Cast: Cocoa Brown, Kent Faulcon, Brad James, Jason Olive, Crystle Stewart,
Michael Jai White, Tasha Smith, Tyrell Lewis, Chevy Lamont Cofield, Kiki
Haynes, Chandra Currelley-Young, Cedric Stewart
Synopsis: A situation comedy that follows the zany and often tumultuous rela-
tionship of a lovesick married couple.

LOVE THY NEIGHBOR (2011–2017)
Networks: OWN and TBS
Genre: Comedy
Executive Producers: **Tyler Perry** and Ozzie Areu
Producers: Mark E. Swinton and Will Areu
Director: **Tyler Perry**
Cast: Palmer Williams Jr., Kendra C. Johnson, Jonathan Chase, Zulay Henao,
Patrice Lovely, Andre Hall, Darmirra Brunson, Tony Grant
Synopsis: A situation comedy revolving around family matriarch and diner
owner, Hattie Mae Love, and her middle-class family's daily triumphs and
struggles.

THE HAVES AND THE HAVE NOTS (2013–2018)
Network: OWN
Genre: Drama, Crime, Mystery

Executive Producers: **Tyler Perry** and Ozzie Areu
Producers: Mark E. Swinton, Will Areu, and Stefi Weaver
Director: **Tyler Perry**
Cast: John Schneider, Tika Sumpter, Aaron O'Connell, Peter Parros, Crystal Fox, Gavin Houston, Angela Robinson, Renee Lawless, Tyler Lepley, Eva Tamargo
Synopsis: Series follows three families and their lifestyles and values as they intersect with one another in Savannah, Georgia.

IF LOVING YOU IS WRONG (2014–2016)
Network: OWN
Genre: Drama
Executive Producers: **Tyler Perry** and Ozzie Areu
Producers: Mark E. Swinton and Will Areu
Director: **Tyler Perry**
Cast: Edwina Findley Dickerson, Aiden Turner, Joel Rush, Amanda Clayton, Zulay Henao, April Parker Jones, Heather Hemmens, Charles Malik Whitfield, Matt Cook, Octavio Pizano, Ryan Haake, Eltony Williams, Denzel Wells, Chase Wainscott, Dawan Owens, Tiffany Haddish, Clayton Landey, Ashlyn Areu
Synopsis: Series focuses on the lives and relationships of a group of five husbands and wives who live on the same street.

TOO CLOSE TO HOME (2016–2017)
Network: TLC
Genre: Drama
Executive Producers: **Tyler Perry** and Ozzie Areu
Producer: Mark E. Swinton
Director: **Tyler Perry**
Cast: Brooke Anne Smith, Charles Justo, Danielle Savre, Brad Benedict, Robert Craighead, Nick Ballard, Justin Gabriel, Kelly Sullivan, Brock O'Hurn, Nelson Estevez, Alpha Trivette, Heather Locklear
Synopsis: The series follows a young woman from a working-class life who, after having an affair with the president of the United States, becomes the center of a political scandal. When the scandal erupts, she returns to her old life.

THE PAYNES (2018–)
Network: OWN
Genre: Comedy
Executive Producer: **Tyler Perry**
Producer: **Tyler Perry**
Director: **Tyler Perry**

Cast: China Anne McClain, Jackée Harry, Lance Gross, Allen Payne, Demetria McKinney, Cassi Davis, Stephanie Charles, Sanai Vitoria, Larramie Doc Shaw, LaVan Davis, Markice Moore, JD McCrary

Synopsis: The Paynes try to enjoy their retirement to Florida until a real estate deal throws their life into a tailspin.

Stage Plays

I KNOW I'VE BEEN CHANGED (1998)

Genres: Comedy, Drama

Director: **Tyler Perry**

Playwright: **Tyler Perry**

Producer: **Tyler Perry**

Cast: **Tyler Perry**, Shirley Marie Graham, Ann Nesby, Jamecia Bennett, Chandra Currelley-Young, Latrice Pace, Ryan Shaw, Carl Pertile, Jasmine Ross, Quan Howell

Synopsis: A story of critical issues including child abuse and rape and how they are overcome by a strong belief in God.

DIARY OF A MAD BLACK WOMAN (2001)

Genre: Comedy, Drama

Director: **Tyler Perry**

Playwright: **Tyler Perry**

Executive Producer: **Tyler Perry**

Producer: **Tyler Perry**

Cast: **Tyler Perry**, Marva King, Curtis Blake, Cordell Moore, Tamela Mann, Tunja Robinson, Regina McCrary, Ty London

Synopsis: A couple's seemingly strong marriage crumbles when the wife discovers that her husband has been having an affair and intends to divorce her.

MADEA'S FAMILY REUNION (2002)

Genre: Comedy

Directors: **Tyler Perry** and Elvin Ross

Playwright: **Tyler Perry**

Executive Producer: **Tyler Perry**

Producer: **Tyler Perry**

Cast: Isaac Carree, Sonya T. Evans, D'Atra Hicks, Gary Jenkins, Pebbles Johnson, David Mann, Tamela Mann, Regina McCrary, Terrell Philips, Mike Storm, James Title IV, Zakiya Williams, **Tyler Perry**

Synopsis: The Simmons family has a funeral, a wedding, and a family reunion all in the same weekend, and it is up to matriarch Madea to keep things in order.

I CAN DO BAD ALL BY MYSELF (2002)
Genre: Comedy
Director: **Tyler Perry**
Playwright: **Tyler Perry**
Executive Producer: **Tyler Perry**
Producer: **Tyler Perry**
Cast: Tyga Graham, Kisha Grandy, David Mann, Tamela J. Mann, Elaine O'Neal, **Tyler Perry,** Carl Pertile, Donna Stewart
Synopsis: A woman, Vianne, is fighting to hold on to her husband after being served with divorce papers, not knowing that he has moved in with her sister and they plan to marry. A shocking family secret is later revealed, and the two sisters must come to terms with their family's dark past.

MADEA'S CLASS REUNION (2003)
Genre: Comedy
Director: **Tyler Perry**
Playwright: **Tyler Perry**
Executive Producer: **Tyler Perry**
Producer: **Tyler Perry**
Cast: **Tyler Perry**, Terrell Carter, Chantelle D. Christopher, Chandra Currelley-Young, D'Wayne Gardner, Anselmo Gordon, David Mann, Tamela J. Mann, Ahmed Jamal McGhee, Judy Peterson, Cheryl Pepsii Riley, Pamela Taylor
Synopsis: Running from the law, Madea takes a break to attend her fiftieth class reunion where she manages to teach valuable lessons on the importance of forgiveness and the value of friendship.

MEET THE BROWNS (2004)
Genre: Comedy
Director: **Tyler Perry**
Playwright: **Tyler Perry**
Executive Producer: **Tyler Perry**
Producer: **Tyler Perry**
Cast: Trina Braxton, Terrell Carter, Nicci Gilbert, Euclid Gray, David Mann, Tamela J. Mann, Kendrick Mays, Demetria McKinney, Terrell Philips, Tamika Scott, Ron Clinton Smith, Joyce D. Williams
Synopsis: Pop Brown lived to be 107 years old, and he only left his family $400 to bury him. His funeral brings out the best and the worst of family members.

WHAT'S DONE IN THE DARK (2006)

Genre: Comedy
Playwright: **Tyler Perry**
Director: **Tyler Perry**
Producer: **Tyler Perry**
Cast: Matisha Baldwin, Terrell Carter, Chantell D. Christopher, Chandra Currelley-Young, Ryan Gentles, Dino Hanson, D'Atra Hicks, Christian Keyes, David Mann, Tamela J. Mann, Ahmad Jamal McGhee, Latrice Pace, Shawna Vinson, Michael Burton
Synopsis: Set in a hospital emergency room, three life struggles unfold: a single nurse struggling to make ends meet for herself and her teenage, basketball-playing son; another single nurse who is having an affair with a doctor; and an eccentric hypochondriac patient, Mr. Brown.

MADEA GOES TO JAIL (2006)

Genres: Comedy, Drama, Musical
Director: **Tyler Perry**
Playwright: **Tyler Perry**
Executive Producer: **Tyler Perry**
Producer: **Tyler Perry**
Cast: **Tyler Perry**, Cheryl Pepsii Riley, Cassi Davis, LaVan Davis, Chantell D. Christopher, Christian Keyes, Ryan Gentles, Brian Hurst, Anndretta Lyle, Crystal Collins, Ron Andrews
Synopsis: After all the running from the police and all the arrest warrants, Madea is finally locked up.

WHY DID I GET MARRIED? (2006)

Genres: Comedy, Drama, Musical
Director: **Tyler Perry**
Playwright: **Tyler Perry**
Executive Producer: **Tyler Perry**
Producer: **Tyler Perry**
Cast: Cheryl Pepsii Riley, LaVan Davis, Donna Stewart, Cordell Moore, Greg Stewart, Tony Grant, Demetria McKinney, Beverly Faulks
Synopsis: As he prepares for his annual marriage retreat to his cabin, Poppy reflects on the good old days when he and his now-deceased wife offered words of wisdom to young married couples. The intent of the retreat was always to provide encouragement and inspiration, but this year the truth takes a sharp turn away from inspiration to hard truths.

THE MARRIAGE COUNSELOR (2008)
Genres: Comedy, Drama, Musical
Director: Nzingha Stewart
Playwrights: Lisa McCree and Darin Spencer
Directors: **Tyler Perry** and Chet Brewster
Executive Producers: Tres A. Miah and Rodney Partner
Producer: John Winter
Cast: Tamar Davis, A. T. Grayson, Myra Beasley, Palmer Williams Jr., Tony Grant, Brandi Milton, Timmons Kyle Turret, Stephanie Ferrett, Johnny Gilmore, Nicole Jackson, Jermaine Sellers
Synopsis: A successful marriage counselor does not recognize the issues with her own marriage. An old college flames reenters her life and entices her to leave her husband, home, and practice. Through a series of unpredictable events, she finds that her new life is not as wonderful as she thought it would be.

LAUGH TO KEEP FROM CRYING (2009)
Genre: Comedy
Director: **Tyler Perry**
Playwright: **Tyler Perry**
Executive Producer: **Tyler Perry**
Producers: **Tyler Perry** and Mark E. Swinton
Cast: Cheryl Pepsii Riley, D'Atra Hicks, Chandra Currelley-Young, Tamar Davis, Stephanie Ferrett, Donnie Sykes, Palmer Williams Jr., Anthony Dalton, Wess Morgan, Rachel Richards, Celestino Cornielle
Synopsis: Life's everyday struggles in the inner city are revealed and shared.

MADEA'S BIG HAPPY FAMILY (2010)
Genre: Comedy
Director: **Tyler Perry**
Playwright: **Tyler Perry**
Executive Producer: **Tyler Perry**
Producers: **Tyler Perry**, Ozzie Areu, and Mark E. Swinton
Cast: **Tyler Perry**, Cassi Davis, Chandra Currelley-Young, Cheryl Pepsii Riley, Palmer Williams Jr., Crystal Collins, Tamar Davis, Jeffrey Lewis, Zuri Craig, Brandi Milton, Chontelle Moore, Danny Clay, Rico Ball, Omarr Dixon
Synopsis: A middle-aged single mother has just received a diagnosis of terminal cancer. With Madea's help, she assembles her grown children for one final reunion during which loyalties are tested and secrets are revealed.

A MADEA CHRISTMAS (2011)
Genre: Musical
Director: **Tyler Perry**
Playwright: **Tyler Perry**
Executive Producers: Ozzie Areu and **Tyler Perry**
Producer: **Tyler Perry**
Cast: Cassi Davis, Cheryl Pepsii Riley, **Tyler Perry**, Alexis Jones, Chandra Currelley-Young, Jeffrey Lewis, Maurice Lauchner, Shannon Williams
Synopsis: A wealthy family meet for Christmas and become entangled in family arguments and secrets. It will take Madea to save Christmas and make it into a good time.

AUNT BAM'S PLACE (2011)
Genre: Musical
Director: **Tyler Perry**
Playwright: **Tyler Perry**
Executive Producer: Ozzie Areu
Producer: Mark E. Swinton
Cast: Cassi Davis, Melonie Daniels, Paris Bennett, Jeffrey Lewis, Taral Hicks, Maurice Lauchner, **Tyler Perry**
Synopsis: Baum's favorite nephew-in-law, Stewart, is granted weekend visitation with his children. He and his new wife are thrilled at the chance until Stewart's drunken ex shows up with trouble in mind.

THE HAVES AND THE HAVE NOTS (2011)
Genre: Drama, Crime, Mystery
Director: **Tyler Perry**
Playwright: **Tyler Perry**
Executive Producer: Ozzie Areu
Producer: **Tyler Perry**
Cast: Palmer E. Williams Jr., Patrice Lovely, Tony Hightower, Alexis Jones, Maurice Lauchner, Jeffrey Lewis, Kislyck Halsey
Synopsis: A wealthy family has become complacent with always having everything they want and need. The family often becomes preoccupied with superficial things until they are forced to become involved with their housekeeper.

MADEA GETS A JOB (2012)
Genre: Comedy
Director: **Tyler Perry**

Playwright: **Tyler Perry**

Executive Producer: Ozzie Areu

Producer: **Tyler Perry**

Cast: **Tyler Perry**, Patrice Lovely, Cheryl Pepsii Riley, Chandra Currelley-Young, Melonie Daniels, Tamar Davis, Stephanie Ferret, Tony Grant, Tony Hightower, Alexis Jones, Maurice Lauchner, Jeffrey Lewis

Synopsis: When a judge orders Madea to do twenty hours of community service at a local retirement home, the residents and staff receive Madea's brash dose of truth as she helps the residents realize the importance of family, love, and forgiveness.

MADEA'S NEIGHBORS FROM HELL (2014)

Genres: Comedy, Drama, Musical

Director: **Tyler Perry**

Playwright: **Tyler Perry**

Executive Producers: Ozzie Areu and **Tyler Perry**

Producer: Mark E. Swinton

Cast: Jayna Brown, Cassi Davis, Rhonda Davis, Kimani Jackson, Wess Morgan, **Tyler Perry**, Chelsea Reynolds, David Stewart, Dathan Thigpen

Synopsis: Madea and Aunt Bam are pitted against some troubling new neighbors, a foster mother and her unruly kids.

MADEA'S HELL HATH NO FURY LIKE A WOMAN SCORNED (2014)

Genres: Comedy, Musical

Director: **Tyler Perry**

Playwright: **Tyler Perry**

Executive Producers: Ozzie Areu, Will Areu, and **Tyler Perry**

Producer: Mark E. Swinton

Cast: Olrick Johnson, Patrice Lovely, Cheryl Pepsii Riley, Muhammad Ayers, Monica Blaire, Zebulon Ellis, Ray Lavender

Synopsis: A love affair goes bad and reveals that you can't scorn a woman and think you've accomplished something.

MADEA ON THE RUN (2017)

Genres: Comedy, Drama, Romance

Director: **Tyler Perry**

Playwright: **Tyler Perry**

Executive Producers: Ozzie Areu and **Tyler Perry**

Producer: Mark E. Swinton

Cast: **Tyler Perry**, Cassi Davis, Tony Hightower, Maurice Lauchner, Rhonda Davis, David Stewart, LaToya London, Claudette Ortiz, Judith Franklin, Dorsey Levens

Synopsis: Madea is on the run from the law again. With no place to turn, she offers to move in with her friend, Aunt Bam, who is recovering from surgery.

Tyler Perry: Interviews

Diary of a Mad Black Woman: An Interview with Tyler Perry

Tonisha Johnson / 2005

From Blackfilm.com, February 2005. Reprinted by permission.

Playwright Tyler Perry exits as Madea stage left to the right onto the big screen. In his play-turned-film, Perry mixes drama and comedy like magic. Making the audience feel wounded and cared for with hilarious anecdotes along the way.

Tonisha Johnson: Was it your idea to turn this play into a movie?
Tyler Perry: When I was writing the play, I thought there was so much more of this story that I wanted to tell. So if I ever got the opportunity to tell the rest of the story I would. And when the opportunity came up, I thought, it has to be *Diary*. It's got to be *Diary*.

TJ: How was the casting done for this film?
TP: Kimberly was first. Every time I would write and I'd get stuck with a scene, I would go, Aw, man, who would do this? So I called Reuben Cannon, who actually did the casting, and I said, "Do you think Kimberly would do this?" And he said, "Well you know she's very selective." So we sent her the material, and she read it and said, "Yeah, I'll do it." That flowed for me. After Kimberly everybody else came. Of course, Shemar being Orlando, there's something in him that a lot of people don't know. That when he comes from in here [taps his chest] like he does in his films . . . when he proposed in that room the entire set was silent. He nailed it. It was really powerful. So those guys were the easy ones. Charles was the hard one. We went through three different guys with Charles. Until we got to the guy that was supposed to play Charles. He was supposed to play him so much that he just happened to be sitting on a plane next to Reuben Cannon going to Vegas. They had a conversation, and Reuben was like . . . you're who we've been looking for. So

he says, "What about Steve Harris?" I said. "*The Practice* guy? Why didn't we think of this?" So, he is Charles. He made you hate him.

TJ: In the beginning of the film, you have Helen [Kimberly Elise] being dragged out by her husband . . .
TP: Yes. That needed to be established to determine why she was so angry. I lessened it. I took a lot of the stuff out of it because I didn't want it too brutal. But when she gets revenge, it makes it that much more powerful.

TJ: Often in films you find that black cast members are beaten, and then the black community has to rise above that. What's your take on that type of casting?
TP: I wanted to make sure that we were all represented well. Not just the females but the males as well. If I'm going to show the bad side of what we can be, then I'm going to show the good side of what we can be.

TJ: Where does your inspirational creativity derive from?
TP: It comes from me . . . from everywhere.

TJ: How did you come about writing plays?
TP: I was watching the *Oprah* show, and she said it was cathartic to write stuff down. That was when I was about eighteen or nineteen years old. And I guess I have been writing since then, that day. I had written about a lot of stuff I had been through. It was a lot of different characters with different names, and a friend of mine said, "Wow, this would be a really good play." And I said, "Maybe that's what it really is," and that's how I fell into my destiny. It's been a hundred miles an hour ever since.

TJ: How much adlibbing did you add to the film?
TP: There was a whole bunch that we cut out. When I'm in the moment in the scene, I'm really not myself. Even Uncle Joe had some of the funniest stuff. But it will be on the DVD because I wanted the film to stay true to the story of what Helen was.

TJ: Did you ever consider putting a real woman in the role of Madea?
TP: No. That would put me out of a job. The only woman who could be that is my aunt and my mother.

TJ: Most black communities in the South have women of that size. It's the ordinary.

TP: I think that's what makes it so unique because it'd be stuff to find a woman that big. Madea is larger than life, literally. When you see this character . . . she's huge. And that's all a part of the comedy, I think.

TJ: Do you think some people may confuse her to be a real lady?
TP: Well a couple of years on stage people actually thought she was. Especially if you weren't very close.

TJ: What can we expect next from Tyler Perry?
TP: I'm working on *Madea's Family Reunion*. Then I'm going to go completely left and do a story about a jazz singer and a holocaust survivor in the 1940s that I want to do. So we're going into a totally different direction.

TJ: What advice do you have for viewers who aspire to do what you do?
TP: For a lot of people it's a lot of different things. For me if you have a natural talent to do things, then nurture it, educate it into making it better. Do everything you can. It goes back to a passage in the Bible . . . "Your gift will make room for you." And I've always believed that. Whatever your gift is, and it's given to you no matter what's going on in the world, no matter how many singers, no matter how many writers, your gift will make room for you in that situation. So, I always believe that. If it's your gift, nurture it and make it the best that it can be.

TJ: Was this the Hollywood homeless?
TP: No. This is not the Kato Kalin homeless. This is Georgia homeless. It was only a three-month period, and I would stay in a pay-by-the-week hotel when I could. Or I would sleep in my car. There are various degrees to it. It's not out on the street, sleeping in the park.

TJ: Do you think other cultures can be open to this type of film?
TP: I say that all the time. If people can just get past the title and just go in and be open to it . . . it can fit to a lot of possibilities, lots of situations.

Exclusive Interview with Tyler Perry:
Finally Reaping Writeousness

Kathleen Cross / 2005

From RollingOut.com, February 22, 2005. Reprinted by permission.

If success really is the sweetest revenge, anyone who ever did anything wrong to Tyler Perry better recognize that the score has officially been settled—and he has upwards of $65 million in earnings on his side of the scoreboard.

Sweet revenge indeed.

But perhaps what is sweetest is that Perry himself is not at all about vengeance or payback; he's about giving back, giving thanks, and forgiving those who've done him wrong. Think that sounds a little too good to be true? Think again. This thirty-six-year-old actor, playwright, producer, director, and CEO of his own multimillion-dollar company is a walking testimonial to the redemptive and regenerative power of two mighty little "f" words: "faith" and "forgive."

Raised in poverty in New Orleans and subjected to a childhood of constant abuse at the hands of his physically present but emotionally distant father, Perry grew into an unhappy young man whose life was shrouded by anger and resentment.

"My experiences as a kid were horrendous," he says. "And I carried all that pain into my adult life." It wasn't until he was nearly thirty years old that Perry finally began to heal. "I was watching Oprah one day, and she suggested writing in a journal as a way to let go of the past," he recalls. He took Oprah's advice and began a series of journal entries detailing his painful childhood experiences. What he wrote eventually became his first play, *I Know I've Been Changed*, a hilarious and inspiring musical about adult survivors of child abuse who confront their abusers and ultimately find healing.

The experience was cathartic for Perry, who was finally able to let go of the anger and bitterness that had held his spirit captive. "I learned real forgiveness," he explains. "That deep-down forgiveness where you don't hold grudges anymore."

Believing that God was calling him to share what he had written with others in need of healing, Perry saved $12,000, relocated to Atlanta, and rented a theater where he produced, directed, and starred in the first theatrical offering of *I Know I've Been Changed*. Thirty people showed up during the entire weekend run of the play. Perry was beyond devastated. He had quit his job and spent his life savings to do what he was sure God wanted—only to find himself penniless and living on the street. "I asked God if quitting my job was the right thing, and I heard him telling me, yes. I clearly heard his voice telling me, 'Go out and do this play and it'll be okay.'"

After the dismal failure of the play, what followed for Perry was a period of homelessness during which his main priority became easing his hunger and finding a safe place to sleep each night. "I didn't hear from God during that time, and that was the darkest for me," he recalls. "I was so angry; I was so mad at God for leading me out there and then leaving me."

Refusing to yield to anger and doubt, Perry ignored the pleas of friends and family to give up on his play and "get a real job." For the next six years he continued to pursue what he still believed was God's will, working a number of odd jobs to finance his play and drifting in and out of homelessness when he couldn't raise enough money to pay rent. Finally in 1998, Perry staged a production of his musical at the House of Blues in Atlanta, and the venue sold out eight times over. Two weeks later, he presented the play at the 4,500-seat Fox Theatre and sold out that venue twice. *Changed* went on to gross several million dollars, and to this day Perry receives mail from fans around the country who say they've experienced healing through his words—something he always knew his play had the power to do.

"Of course, I understand now what that was," he says of the time he spent suffering and struggling to bring his work to life. "God was preparing me for all that was to come." All that was to come is Perry's characteristically humble way of referring to the enormous success he has achieved since that bleak period in his life. Over the last seven years he has written, produced, directed, and owns all rights to the seven hit plays that have broken box office records across the country and grossed more than $50 million. On his website, www.tylerperry.com, fans can purchase videos and DVDs of the plays—another lucrative arm of Perry's business that brings in several million dollars per year. With titles like *I Can Do Bad All by Myself, Diary of a Mad Black Woman, Madea's Family Reunion, Madea's Class Reunion*, and his latest play, *Madea Goes to Jail*, Perry has attracted a following of staunch supporters who stand in line again and again and place their names on DVD waiting lists to experience his unique and controversial brand of urban theater.

Especially popular with Perry's fans is his stage portrayal of Madea Simmons, a sixty-eight-year-old grandmother who packs a pistol in her purse, smokes marijuana, and says she'll consider going to church "when they get a smoking section."

Donning a housedress, fake breasts, and a healthy coating of Maybelline, the six-foot-five Perry delights audiences with Madea's crude and raucous sense of humor. In between cussing, fussing, and embarrassing her loved ones, Madea offers lessons on self-esteem, parenting, forgiveness, and faith in God. Madea's fans will be happy to know that she is making her February 25 feature-film debut in the screen adaptation of Perry's wildly popular play *Diary of a Mad Black Woman*. The film stars Kimberly Elise, Shemar Moore, Steve Harris, Cicely Tyson, and, of course, Tyler Perry, who plays three characters. The movie, directed by Darren Grant, weaves together a brilliant mix of drama and comedy to tell the story of Helen McCarter (Kimberly Elise), who is dumped by her husband after eighteen years of marriage and must fight the urge to exact revenge. It is a hilarious and ultimately heartwarming story of marital betrayal, forgiveness, self-love, and the importance of family.

Bypassing the Hollywood studios who were put off by the title and too eager to modify the storyline, Perry teamed up with producer Reuben Cannon (who brought audiences the film version of T. D. Jakes's *Woman Thou Art Loosed*) to ensure that *Diary* stayed true to its themes of forgiveness and redemption. "I own my brand," says Perry of his experience meeting with studio execs. "They want to put me in a room with a bunch of people who don't look like me and write for me? There's no amount of money that's going to make me walk away from the thing that I know works. This is my calling—to speak to an entire generation. That's a huge responsibility, and I've got to protect it and keep it."

Perry knows the power to say no to Hollywood money is rare for urban filmmakers, and he gives full credit for that power to that sixty-eight-year-old grandmother named Madea. "Madea's fan base . . . put pressure on me to stay real," he explains. Though Madea is fictional, there is no doubt that she represents a real influence on the man who created her. "Madea is my mother, my aunt, and all the women in my life who loved me enough to speak their minds," says Tyler. "She teaches us how to forgive, how to let things go, and how to move on."

When it comes to forgiving and moving on, Tyler Perry has definitely taken Madea's advice to heart. He now lives in a lavishly decorated, $5 million mansion surrounded by perfectly manicured grounds complete with two secluded prayer gardens. And when it comes to prayer, Perry says he has learned a powerful lesson about how to approach God with his needs. "I don't ask God for anything. I stopped asking for things a long time ago. Even when people come to me and ask me to pray for them, my prayer for them is, 'God, let your will be done.'"

Of his extravagant home, Perry says he believes his house should make a statement to those who doubt the power of faith and forgiveness. "I want people to know what God can do when you believe." Despite the luxury surrounding him, Perry says he has never lost his commitment to love, touch, and heal others.

"Cicely Tyson said something to me I will never forget," he offers humbly. "'When the thing you do starts to serve you more than it serves the people—you are no longer a servant.'" Asked if he is proud of himself, Tyler responds calmly, "I'm proud of the body of work I've produced. I'm still working on me."

The Many Faces of Tyler Perry

Kristi Watts / 2006

From *The 700 Club*, 2006. Reprinted by permission.

His name is Tyler Perry, and he's taking Hollywood by storm.

Tyler not only acts in his movies and plays. He writes, directs, produces, and composes for some of them too!

His first two films, *Diary of a Mad Black Woman* and *Madea's Family Reunion*, made a smash hit at the box office.

He's a man of many faces. His most famous is a sixty-something, tell-it-like-it-is woman named Madea.

So, who is this man behind these characters? And what's the key to his success? When *700 Club* producer Kristi Watts talked with Tyler, she found a strong man of faith who uses laughter as a means to lead people to faith, forgiveness, and fullness in God.

"I try to write from a point of view with my faith being always present and always there," Tyler tells the *700 Club*. "I don't want to write characters where everyone is saved. So this Madea character for me is not saved. It's been important to me that she not be because what it has been is this great tool to draw people in. They come in laughing, joking, and having a great time, but before you know it, I've planted seeds of life that hopefully fall on good ground for a lot of people."

Tyler's childhood taught him some harsh, early lessons.

"The heart of who I am as a person and as a man is forgiveness," he explains, "after forgiving my father for a lot of things that were done when I was child."

As if it was a story line from one of his own plays, Tyler describes a childhood filled with both physical and verbal abuse at the hands of his own father.

"To understand it from a child's point of view, when you're looking at this man who is supposed to be your protector and take care of you, and he's the one that's causing the most pain in your life, of course that is difficult."

As an adult, Tyler found it cathartic to write down his feelings of pain and rejection. Those journal entries turned into plays.

"My first show was called *I Know I've Been Changed* in '92. I tried to do this show for years and years. It kept failing over and over and over again. Every time I went out to do the show, nobody showed up. I was like, 'What is this about?' And I became angry.

"I had a chance in '98. This was going to be my last show. I wasn't doing another play. I was twenty-eight years old at the time. I said, 'This is enough. You need to get a good job like your momma said and get you some benefits.' The rent couldn't be paid, and I was sitting there going, 'God, I don't know what You're doing, but I praise You anyway. I'm thankful for it. Even though I didn't hear from You, I don't know what's going on, I'm still grateful.'

"I'm talking to God, and I say, 'Every time I went out to do something You tell me, nobody shows up.' So I'm complaining, and the Spirit comes over me. I start crying. I got so calm. He said, 'Look out the window.' There was a line around the corner trying to get in. [I thought,] Okay, this is bigger than anything I could imagine.

"I learned to surrender, which has been the most difficult thing I've had to learn in my life Not my will, but His will be done."

Part of surrendering meant forgiving his father.

"If you don't truly forgive, you hold yourself back. You know the Bible says you need to forgive so that the Father can forgive you, which is totally what I believe.

"Now we have a very good relationship because I know I've forgiven him. I can sit in the room with him and talk and laugh and have a good time because there is nothing there. There is nothing I'm harboring. The reason I was able to do that was I realized the effect that it had on me."

Tyler believes his unsuccessful years could have been due to his unforgiveness.

"I think that's why the show wasn't doing well up until '98, because I hadn't forgiven him up until the time," Tyler says. "There was so much anger and frustration, and I was self-sabotaging so many things without even knowing it because I hadn't let that go. But once I learned that, [I was] free to go on."

These days, much of his work is a personal diary of his own life lessons—lessons he had to learn in order to handle the success he's experiencing today.

"It made me know all of those times of being homeless and out on the street He was proving me to see, 'Will you compromise?' So I went to Hollywood and they were saying, 'We want you to change this, this, and this.' Everything was 'no,' because I knew not to compromise. What I had learned from that experience is that He will see me through."

It's his obedience to the will of God that proves to be the key to Perry's success. That success continues with his first book which has already topped the *New York Times* bestsellers list.

So what's in store for Tyler Perry?

"A lot more good days and happiness," he says. "Happiness for me is totally just being at peace knowing that everything I'm doing God is pleased with that. It's complete peace for me."

Tyler Perry *The Family That Preys* Interview

Kam Williams / 2008

From NewsBlaze.com, September 9, 2008. Reprinted by permission.

A Visit to Tyler Perry's *House of Payne*

Tyler Perry's path from the perilous streets of New Orleans to the heights of Hollywood is a unique and inspiring version of the American Dream. Born into poverty and raised in a household scarred by abuse, from a young age, Perry found a way to summon the strength, faith, and perseverance that would later form the foundation of his award-winning plays, films, books, and TV show, *House of Payne*.

Tyler credits a simple piece of advice from Oprah Winfrey for setting his meteoric rise in motion. Encouraged to keep a diary of his daily thoughts and experiences, he began writing a series of soul-searching letters to himself—reflections full of pain, forgiveness, and, in time, a healing catharsis. Along the way, he spent a challenging period homeless, sleeping in seedy motels and in his car, but his faith in God and, in turn, in himself, only got stronger. Forging a powerful relationship with the church, he kept writing until his perseverance paid off, and the rest is history.

Here, the prolific and versatile Renaissance man shares his thoughts about his latest production, *The Family That Preys*, a movie which he wrote, produced, directed, and costars in.

KW: Hey Tyler, thanks so much for the time.
TP: Hi Kam, good to talk to you again.

KW: Where did you get the idea for *The Family That Preys*?
TP: I was just going through some things in my life I was having issues with. This newfound fame was really starting to smother me, and somebody asked me, "Are you living or just existing?" I thought "Wow!" and I started writing. And this film came out of that. At the time I heard Lee Ann Womack singing "I Hope You Dance,"

and it really touched me. When you watch the movie, towards the end you'll see a Gladys Knight remake of the song at the moment that the film takes on the personality of, "Live! Life is short! Live every day like it's your last."

KW: I love your work and admire all that you've accomplished, which always makes me wonder how your brain works differently from the rest of ours.
TP: You know what I think it is? I just may be a little bit more inquisitive. For example, when someone tells me no, I ask, "Why?" like I did with *House of Payne*, which will be going into syndication on the twenty-second of September. Originally, they told me that I had to shoot one show a week, because that's how it's done in Hollywood. But when I questioned that, nobody could tell me why. The same thing happened when they told me you could only shoot one movie per year. When I asked, "Why?" nobody could give me an answer. So, I believe it's the inquisitiveness which breeds everything else that comes along with it. I just ask a lot of questions.

KW: Do you see *The Family That Preys* as being more of a mainstream movie, or do you see it as appealing to your regular demographic?
TP: I think it's definitely going to appeal to my same audience. But do you know what I was doing? I was just telling a story. When I imagined the first two characters, I saw Alfre Woodard and Kathy Bates. And then when I started developing their relationships, all these kids came out of it. So, I didn't set out to go mainstream with this film. That wasn't my intention. This is just me telling a story.

KW: We recently passed the third anniversary of Hurricane Katrina. Have you had an opportunity to go back to your hometown, New Orleans, lately to check on the progress of the recovery?
TP: I have, and nothing's changed. Nothing's changed. The only thing different is that people are being evicted from those FEMA trailers.

KW: Is there any question that no one ever asks you that you wish someone would?
TP: Yeah, "Can I pay for dinner?" Nobody ever asks me that.

KW: The Tasha Smith question: Are you ever afraid?
TP: Certainly, there are times when I feel fear, but I don't live in it. I think as human beings we all feel fear, but I refuse to live in it. So, it doesn't last very long.

KW: Have you ever been disappointed?
TP: Certainly, I've been disappointed a lot. But you take your disappointments

and you learn from them. If you learn a lesson from them, then you're okay, because as long as you're human there will be disappointments.

KW: The Columbus Short question: Are you happy?
TP: Yeah, I can honestly say I'm truly, truly dancing and living my life. And I think this film was my catharsis to getting there.

KW: Bookworm Troy Johnson asks: What was the last book you read?
TP: I haven't read a book in a very, very long time, because when I'm writing I don't like to see other people's work. I don't want to see something great and not be able to use it, and I don't want to have any subconscious influences. So, it's been an extremely long time. I think the last book I read might have been Maya Angelou's *Hallelujah!*

KW: Music maven Heather Covington asks: What are you listening to nowadays?
TP: Everything from Lee Ann Womack to Jay-Z's "30's the new 20."

KW: Who are you supporting for president?
TP: Barack. Absolutely Barack!

KW: How do you want to be remembered?
TP: As a person who made people laugh but inspired us all to be better.

KW: What message do you want people to get from *The Family That Preys*?
TP: That every day is a gift. Life is short, so live it like it's your last.
Thank you, my friend, and I'll talk to you soon.

KW: Well, thanks again for the interview, and good luck with the film.

Q&A: Tyler Perry

Matthew Belloni and Stephen Galloway / 2009

From the *Hollywood Reporter*, February 18, 2009. Reprinted by permission of Matthew Belloni, Editorial Director.

He survived abuse as a child and lived in his car at one point. Then Tyler Perry channeled his emotions into a series of popular stage plays and movies featuring his mad, black alter-ego Madea. Now Perry, thirty-nine, helps finance and maintains total creative control of his films, his two TV shows, and, as of October, his very own studio just outside Atlanta, where he is based. With Oprah Winfrey as a role model, he's looking to grow his empire, recently launching 34th Street Prods. to help bring films he loves to his loyal audience—including the Sundance hit *Precious: Based on the Novel By Sapphire*. In advance of the Friday release of his latest film, *Madea Goes to Jail*, Perry sat down in the spacious, minimalist living room of his Hollywood Hills home to chat with THR's Matthew Belloni and Stephen Galloway.

The Hollywood Reporter: How do you describe your filmmaking style?
Tyler Perry: My stories are usually pretty predictable. The dialogue is always very simple because I am very aware of who I am speaking to. My audience is from 2- and 3-year-olds all the way up to 90, so I'm not trying to tell any extremely stylistic, artistic stories.

THR: Why has your audience been ignored by Hollywood?
TP: For the most part people speak from their own experiences, and in Hollywood there have not been a lot of African Americans who have been able to tell their stories unfiltered, unedited, with no notes, and bring (them) directly to the people. That's why I love my relationship with Lionsgate: It's a no-note, we-don't-show-up-to-the-set relationship. I bring them a finished film and we test it and it usually does extremely well.

THR: The studios do so much research about who audiences are and what they want, and this is an audience that for many years was just missed. How is that?

TP: Even from my first movie (*Diary of a Mad Black Woman*), the tracking was way off. They have gotten better with tracking and understanding my films, but if you're not a part of (the community), you can't really get the information. I don't know what it's like to be Japanese. But if I was there in the culture I could get some sort of understanding. I think you need to be in the culture to understand it. I'm really only beginning to wrap my brain around how Hollywood can be so insulated from the rest of the world. There is Hollywood and then there is New York—and then America is in the middle. I've been to every major city in this country, with the exception of the Dakotas, I think, and we would sell shows out—30,000–40,000 people a week coming in the doors. People find this hard to believe, and most of it was sold by e-mail before we even got to the city. I have the box office record at the Kodak (Theatre, in Hollywood). I had eighteen or nineteen shows there that have all sold out.

THR: What is your exact demographic? We know it is largely black women, but is there anything more specific?

TP: It's about 50 percent Christian churchgoing. It depends on what part of the country I'm in. If I'm in the Bible Belt it's 90 percent churchgoing. If I'm up north in Newark it may be 30 percent, so it depends on where you are. I used to adjust the shows to where I am. If I was in the Bible Belt I made it more Christian, God-themed. If I was up north I could get away with saying "ass" a little more. I would say 75–80 percent women, 10–20 percent men, and about 5 percent children. What I've learned is you treat the women right, and they bring everybody else.

THR: Has the audience changed at all since you started making films?

TP: My last tour was in 2004–5, and it started to change. It was the first time I was onstage, and I could look out in the audience. And there would be maybe five white people or Hispanic. Then there were 600–700 or 1,000 in the audience. The videos (of the plays) had gotten out there.

THR: In Hollywood, the conventional wisdom is, "Don't fund your own projects." You defied that. Why?

TP: When I came into Hollywood, I was doing extremely well. Before I even had a film, my shows were approaching $100 million on tour. I didn't come in saying, "Give me this money so that I can do a film," because when that happens you lose all creative control. The money is not as important to me as the creative control. So I have to fund it for that to happen, just as I've done it in television.

THR: You just announced eighty episodes of *Meet the Browns* on TBS, on top of the hundred episodes of *House of Payne*. You're paying for the production?

TP: It's all Tyler Perry Studios, which has allowed me complete creative control. I was willing to take the risk because I know this audience. I know that if I send an e-mail, if I ask them to watch, they do.

THR: What is your long-term plan?

TP: I'd love to do a deal with Sony to do a two-hander (acting in a movie with a costar) with someone who has international appeal. Not a *Madea* movie, not a Tyler Perry movie, but just a movie. That's why I took the role in (May's) *Star Trek*, just to see how that goes. Can I do this? Can I be on somebody else's set? (Once) I yelled, "Cut!" on the set, and the whole room turned and looked at (director J. J. Abrams). It was my fault. I was screwing up the line, and I yelled, "Cut!" Everybody in the room was like, "Who does this kid think he is?" They all look at J. J., and J. J. had this big smile on his face. (I saw) what it's like to work with other people and how it would work for me, and it was fantastic.

THR: Could you see yourself collaborating more in the future?

TP: I don't consider myself as a director. I'm always going to write in my brand and direct for my brand. But I could see myself as an actor for hire. Please, it'd be a vacation, are you kidding me?

THR: Why did you say Sony?

TP: Will Smith invited me to Europe and took me to three different countries. He said, "This is so possible." He has had success with (Sony). And looking at their operation and what's happening with them—it could be Fox too—but we need somebody with huge international arm, and Lionsgate doesn't have that.

THR: Are you making a deal with one of those studios?

TP: We're in the beginning stages of figuring out what's the project, what to do, and where to go.

THR: But with Will Smith as the major exception, African American–themed films tend not to do well overseas.

TP: Why do people say that? Will Smith showed me the data. The dubbers are important, the way it's marketed is important. Each country is a whole other world, so I think (my) films could do well there. But there are so many variables. The Wayans brothers have done well—*White Chicks* and *Scary Movie*. If you find someone who is willing to invest in all areas—marketing, dubbing, everything—so that it's familiar to the actual country—it can work.

THR: Why did you and Oprah Winfrey decide to put your names behind *Push*?
TP: (Lionsgate execs) called me from Sundance. They brought it to me and I watched it. I called Oprah and said, "You've got to watch this film," and she said, "I've got it; I've had it for a month." So she watched it and then we were like, "What can we do to make this film get to an audience?" Mo'Nique should win the Academy Award. Mariah Carey is so freakin' great in this movie, and she is unrecognizable.

THR: Is it Lionsgate's film or could it possibly go to the Weinstein Co.?
TP: It's Lionsgate's film. 34th Street has a first-look deal with them. There are two brains at work here. There is 34th Street that is going to do more of these *Push* kind of movies, more artistic kinds of things that people don't expect me to do. Then there is the Tyler Perry–branded movie that is specifically branded as simple stories, funny, family, faith-based, no incredible plot twists. It is very important to me to show children what a whole family unit looks like. If you see the worst of what a man can be, as I did growing up, you can also see the best a man can be.

THR: Where do you get your ability to create stories that resonate with women?
TP: My mother and father. I would wake up and there were always strangers in the house. If somebody needed to be taken in she would take them in and feed them. And watching the stuff that my father did and the kind of man he was, I think it would turn a child into one of two things. It would either make him a womanizer or it would make him very sympathetic, and I went the sympathetic route. (My mother) took me everywhere with her to protect me from him. Everywhere. I went to the hair salon; I went into the women's restroom. I went to the Lane Bryant stores. When you're sitting around on the floor, there is no better viewpoint; children can see everything. That's why I like to drop the camera low in a lot of angles to see what kids see. When you're in that situation and you're watching that, it has a profound effect on you.

THR: What was the thinking behind creating your own studio, how has it impacted Atlanta, and can you make a go of it in the long term?
TP: Oh yes, certainly. The financial impact is tremendous in the town. So much so that they passed this 30 percent tax break. There is a positive and a negative about working there. The negative is the talent—not just actors but everybody. If they're not there, they have to be brought in. But the positive is the sense of community and family and the tremendous amount of respect and pride there. So much so that all of the unions—except the WGA—were so on my side when I started. They helped me build it—SAG, Teamsters, all of them—because of the pride in it.

THR: Why was there that conflict with the WGA last year?

TP: You know what, it was resolved in the end, and I was very happy with the way it was resolved. And (thanks to) the NAACP for stepping in. I had been trying to negotiate with the WGA for five months. Five months trying to get them to do a deal because I wanted to have better writers on (*House of Payne*). But I couldn't—being an independent, a person who is not Sony and not Disney—I could not agree to what they were asking me to pay. And because I wouldn't agree to it, all hell broke loose. All I was trying to do was get a fair deal, and in the end I got a fantastic deal that I'm very happy with.

THR: Walk us through your creative process.

TP: Months before I ever sit down to write, the story will be there in my mind. And I rarely ever write two drafts. It's a three-week process when I actually sit down to write. I see the scenes; I dream the scenes. I went out to a restaurant the other day, and I talked to the maître d' for forty-five minutes because he completely intrigued me. He was from Detroit and he talked with this accent and he was Middle Eastern. All of the richness. I just listened to him, and I came back. And I had a whole twenty pages just from the thought of who he was.

THR: Your next film is shooting in March. What can you tell us about it?

TP: I don't know the title, but it's got a little bit of Madea in it. It's about a woman who is living her complete life, and she is just happy. She works in a club; she's in her twenties; she isn't thinking about anything. Her sister was strung out on drugs and died, so her mother is raising the children. And they haven't found the mother for four days. Then the kids find out that their grandmother was on the way to work and died on the bus, and nobody knew it. And this girl, who's twenty-five, twenty-six and singing at this club, doing ladies night, open mike, is shocked to realize that she has to raise these children. It changes her life and the children's lives.

THR: Who do you see as the girl?

TP: Even if she doesn't do it, I see Jennifer Hudson as this girl.

THR: Do you read the feedback your fans give you on your message board?

TP: I do, I have to. I had a character say "biatch" in *Meet the Browns*, and the board went crazy. "My children are watching; how dare you!" Instant. That was me testing to see how much I could get away with, how far I could go. They are my lifeline.

THR: What are they going to think of *Star Trek*?

TP: I don't know. I don't know what I'm going to think of *Star Trek*? (Laughs)

THR: What's an average day like for you?

TP: I'm usually up at about 6 or 7 working out. And then I get to the studio. We will do a table read in the morning and block the show, and then I'll leave and let them rehearse it. I'll go up to the office; I'll do some writing, some working, take meetings and then come back at 2:30 to shoot the show. The show is done by 5. If I'm shooting a movie at the same time, I'll leave the show at 5 and go to the set or go next door to whatever stage the movie is on and work until like midnight. I can do that for about ninety days, and then I need a long break.

THR: You seem pretty relaxed for a guy with so much going on.

TP: I'm not that stressing guy. But this year we are going to do three films and the eighty episodes of *Meet the Browns*. I'll tell you what stresses me, though, is finding the people. I need people who don't have the Hollywood mentality because you tell people who have worked on sitcoms that we are doing three or four shows a week, and they go, "Are you crazy?" But you tell a person who has never done it, and they think, "Wow, cool, this is the way it's done."

THR: How do you juggle the artistic and the business sides of what you do? Is there a danger that the more you focus on marketing to your audience, you will pull away from purely doing what you want to artistically?

TP: No, my brain has that side. Like an architect. I have to force myself when I'm doing one to not think about the others. When I'm writing, I don't want to think, "Oh, let's see what's going to work to make this more appealing or more commercial."

THR: The e-mails you send to your fans are very candid. How much does your relationship with them translate into the kind of work you create?

TP: I'm very aware of it because I know what I represent to them. I am them. I am what they went through. And I was where a lot of them are. I've been through things that a lot of the people who support me have been through or are going through, and I represent hope to them. That is a tremendous burden because you're living this very high-profile life but you are also very human.

THR: Ten or twelve years ago you were living in your Geo Metro. How did you project your life would turn out at that point?

TP: I was so angry. I'm still angry at my father, and I still have so much to work through. I think I was more concerned about working through things for myself than what my life would be. And that's where my first play came from. It came out of me trying to find a catharsis. In this movie *Precious*, Paula Patton's character says to the lead character, "Write." This girl is going through all kinds of stuff, and she says, "Write, just write," which was really touching because it was the writing that made me say, "I can be OK."

THR: Looking ahead, where do you want to be in five or ten years?
TP: You know, I got really depressed after my studio opened because I realized it was a major goal that I had obtained. I said, "OK, now what?" I'd like to own a network. Every time you turn it on, whether you're watching for five minutes or an hour, you're inspired. Even if it's just children laughing in a commercial. I'd like to continue to grow this brand while at the same time have an actual acting career outside of Madea.

THR: Oprah is starting her own network. Is she still a major role model?
TP: Oh sure. Bill Cosby, Oprah. Definitely Oprah. I just looked at the model, looked at the things that she did and how she did it.

THR: What's the most memorable advice she's given you?
TP: I'd only met her once, and I'm in Las Vegas walking down the street. And the phone rings, and she says, "Just saw *Diary*. Hold on to yourself." And that has come back to me because learning how to fly in thin air can be tough. So it's always, "Hold on to yourself, remember who you are, no matter what anybody says. No matter what attacks come, hold on to yourself."

THR: Are you waiting to see how Oprah does with her OWN network?
TP: I was on to it before she ever announced it. (Laughs) She announced it the day we were talking to somebody about it, and I was like, "Aw, man."

THR: So you're already planning that?
TP: Yeah, we've been talking for a while about it.

THR: You have some charitable interests too, don't you?
TP: Quite a bit. This year we are launching the Tyler Perry Foundation, which will fund a lot of charities that involve children and the elderly. My goal is to match whatever donations come in to it. We built twenty houses for victims of (Hurricane) Katrina, homeless shelters for thousands of people in Atlanta. We've done some things with children's shelters. I want it to be self-sufficient and fund a lot of charities because these times are very difficult for charities.

THR: There are a couple film projects that you've been connected with, *Jazz Man's Blues* and *Georgia Sky*. What are they?
TP: *Georgia Sky* is going to be a direct-to-DVD series that is for teenage girls mostly. I didn't write it, somebody named Stephanie Perry wrote it. She sold

200,000–300,000 books in the South, and I was like, I want to be involved in that. *Jazz Man's Blues* is a movie that I wrote in 1995 about a Holocaust survivor and a jazz singer. I've wanted to do it for a long, long time, and I finally realized this year it's been fear that has kept me from doing it.

THR: Fear of what?

TP: Not being able to direct it. I look at real directors—you know, Oliver Stone, Spike Lee, those people—they can do epic war stories. It takes place in World War II. I (need to) learn more about cameras, lighting, and things like that. I called (director) John Sayles about doing it. He only does his own projects, but he gave me fantastic advice.

THR: Black audiences spend $8 billion a year on entertainment. Are they well served?

TP: No, absolutely not. I'm not an expert on this—and the black dollar is spread over so much, there is so much entertainment—but when it's focused it's very powerful.

THR: What do you think of the term "urban entertainment"?

TP: When I started doing plays it was called the Chitlin Circuit, and I was very offended by that. Then I studied it and I realized what it was. The Chitlin Circuit was where Ray Charles and Della Reese and all of these people went because they couldn't stay in the white hotels. And it was black people who supported them and made them famous. So I began to have a great affection for the term. I don't use it, but I have a great affection for it. And then somewhere I read that my shows were called "Urban Theater." I don't know where that came from. I guess somebody was trying to elevate the term.

THR: Is having Barack Obama in the White House going to change things for African Americans?

TP: All I can tell you is what it's done for me. I was beginning to see things in black and white, and it was really awful. When my name is mentioned it's "Tyler Perry the African American filmmaker," you know? When Steven Spielberg is mentioned it's not "Steven Spielberg, Jewish filmmaker." Everything started to really affect me. I opened Tyler Perry Studios on October 3. The first African American individual to own a major film/television studio, and the press was difficult to get. And I just thought, why is there no interest? Then (on Election Night) I sat on the bed with tears falling out of my eyes because I realized that this man was judged on the content of his character, period. There are millions of people out there who don't see black and white, and I've got to stop seeing it.

Tyler Perry's Amazing Journey to the Top: He Is One of America's Top Filmmakers, Yet Few Have Ever Heard of Him

Byron Pitts / 2009

From *60 Minutes*, October 22, 2009. Reprinted by permission.

What filmmaker has had five movies open number one at the box office in the last four years? Spielberg, Tarantino, Scorsese? No. This record belongs to Tyler Perry, one of the biggest names in the movie business. Yet most Americans have never heard of him.

His eight films have grossed more than $418 million, one of the highest average grosses per film in the industry. And they're just part of Perry's multi-million-dollar entertainment empire.

What has made Perry guaranteed box office gold is his devoted audience: largely African American, church-going, working class, and female.

Long ignored by Hollywood, they come to see something they can't get anywhere else: inspirational stories about people like themselves and to laugh at characters like his Madea, the wise-cracking grandmother played by Perry himself.

"Madea is a cross between my mother and my aunt. She's the type of grandmother that was on every corner when I was growing up," Perry told correspondent Byron Pitts. "She smoked. She walked out of the house with her curlers and her muumuu and she watched everybody's kids. She didn't take no crap. She's a strong figure where I come from. In my part of the African American community. And I say that because I'm sure that there are some other parts of the African American community that may be looking at me now going, 'Who does he think he's speaking of?' But, for me, this woman was very, very visible."

That's what Perry's work is all about—reflecting a world his audience relates to. And they show up in droves.

"It's been written that Madea is one of the top ten grossing women actresses in the country," Pitts noted.

"They weren't serious when they wrote that. I mean, come on," Perry said, laughing. "Come on."

But he acknowledged that Madea has done very well; so have his other popular characters, like the flamboyant Leroy Brown.

But it's not just comedy. Perry's work is a gumbo of melodrama, social commentary, and inspiration. It's a formula that intentionally targets women.

"You're always gonna see a person of faith. Nine times out of ten, it'll be a woman who has problems, who has lost faith or lost her way," Perry explained. "There's always gonna be a moment of redemption somewhere for someone."

And then there are the grittier, darker elements: the violence, especially directed at women and children, sex and child abuse, prostitution and drugs use. But there is always a fairy tale ending, a happy marriage, a reconciliation—often delivered with a dose of Gospel music.

Although Perry's themes are universal, he is not widely known outside of his niche audience.

"The average American has no idea who you are. How is that possible?" Pitts asked.

"I'll tell you how it's possible. There's this great thing called the Chitlin Circuit, which I started my shows on and back in the day when, you know, Ray Charles and Billie Holiday and Duke Ellington . . . they couldn't get into white establishments, so they went on this circuit and toured. They were huge stars in their own community, you know, and that's pretty much my same story. I was able to build and have this amazing career among my own people, but outside of that, you know, not a lotta people knew who I was," Perry explained.

"Tyler Perry, superstar of the Chitlin Circuit?" Pitts asked.

"Yeah. Superstar of the Chitlin Circuit, I'll take that," Perry replied, laughing.

You realize what a superstar he is and how strongly the audience connects to him when he appears on stage after a performance of one of his plays. Their overwhelming reaction gives you a sense of how passionate they are about him.

But he didn't always get this kind of reaction. He got his start in theater, writing, directing, and producing plays.

His first production, a Gospel musical staged in Atlanta in 1992, bombed. But he kept writing and staging new plays, cultivating his audience. By the late 1990s, the plays were selling out across the country, making big money—more than $75 million.

Perry's goal was to turn those shows into movies. Hollywood's reaction: get lost.

"They didn't open the door. I had to cut a hole in the window to get in," Perry said. "You close the door on me and tell me I can't, I'm gonna find a way to get in."

He found his way in by setting up shop in Atlanta in 2004, where he made his first film, *Diary of A Mad Black Woman*, using his own money.

"He who has the gold makes the rules. If somebody else is gonna give you the money, then, they're gonna be in control. They're gonna own it; they're gonna tell you how it goes. They're gonna give you notes and give you changes. I wasn't willing to do that, so there was no other option for me," Perry told Pitts.

Diary debuted at number one in 2005, stunning Hollywood.

Perry has been surprising Hollywood ever since, doing it his way. He writes, directs, and produces his movies. And all eight of them have been major hits, including his latest, *I Can Do Bad All by Myself*, which opened number one at the box office in September.

Tyler Perry Studios—thirty-one acres of movie and television production facilities - is one of the largest independently owned studios outside of Hollywood. It opened last October, financed by Perry himself, with the profits he has made from his productions.

It's Perry's multi-million-dollar "Magic Kingdom."

"This is the back lot, and I named it 34th Street, as in *Miracle on 34th Street*," Perry explained.

He makes all his films there, releasing two a year; he employs as many as four hundred people. The studio lot has five sound stages, a gym, and even a chapel.

When he is not making movies, this relentless multitasker is running his two hit sitcoms on TBS, *House of Payne* and *Meet the Browns*.

He has total creative control and owns everything he makes.

Perry's huge success has brought him power and even comparisons to Oprah, his friend and mentor. They've teamed up to executive-produce *Precious*, a film about an urban teenage mother battling abuse and illiteracy which opens in November.

"Do not play him small because he is not just some lucky rich Negro-turned-black man," Winfrey said, laughing. "He is not. To be able to take what he saw as an opportunity to reach a group of people and to turn that into this multi-million, soon to be multi-billion-dollar enterprise is what everybody else is trying to do."

Asked what connection she thinks Perry has with African American women, Winfrey told Pitts, "Well, first of all, I think he grew up being raised by strong, black women. And so much of what he does is really in celebration of that. I think that's what Madea really is, a compilation of all those strong black women that I know and maybe you do too. And so the reason it works is because people see themselves."

Perry says he's writing what he knows, writing where he comes from. He grew up working class in a tough New Orleans neighborhood.

"Man, my heart is racing just being here, isn't that crazy?" Perry said, while visiting the old neighborhood with Pitts.

Asked why, Perry said, "I don't have good memories here at all."

But it's those memories, both good and bad, that have inspired much of his work.

Pitts and 60 *Minutes* met two neighbors who reminded us an awful lot of a certain grandmother: Madea.

"These are the kinda women I grew up with," Perry told Pitts.

"And Christian women, Christian women," one of the neighborhood women said.

"And Christian women with guns," Perry joked. "And the people wonder where Madea came from!"

They crossed the street to where Perry used to live. The pain of his past came back. "This is where I grew up. And I have not been in this house in years," Perry said.

In the house, Perry says his father Emmitt repeatedly beat him and his mother Maxine. He describes one time when his father whipped him with a cord until the skin came off his back.

Perry says when his father wasn't beating him, he was belittling him.

He told Pitts his father used to warn his mother about him. "One day I would make her cry, 'cause she would try to protect me from him. 'What the f--- are you protecting him for? What are you protecting him for?' Like, 'This boy is s---. He ain't gonna be s---. One day he gonna make you cry,'" Perry remembered.

He brought us out back, where he showed Pitts the cubbyhole he would escape to from his father's abuse.

"This was my hideout, my safe place, you know," Perry said. "I'd spend all day in there."

"So I had a door there, so I could go in and close myself up, you know, to be okay for a minute. Yeah," he added.

"Your father, it sounds like, can still make you feel like that boy, that little boy. How was that possible?" Pitts asked.

"You'd have to walk that road and be that little boy," Perry said. "A lot of it I've put out of my mind because it was so horrific and so painful that had I not, that's where my imagination was born. When he was losing it and saying all those things, it would—I could absolutely be there in that room with him at the top of his lungs and go somewhere else in my head."

His faith, and his mother, he says, saved him. "Sunday morning she'd take me to church. And this is the only time I saw her smile and happy, so I wanted to know the God, this Christ, that made my mother smile so much."

Perry says he has forgiven his father and come to terms with the abuse. "This is what happens. You let it destroy you or you take it and you use it. I chose to use it and I chose to put in my work and I choose to have it touch and make people understand it," he told Pitts.

Yet there are some who don't understand Perry's work and dismiss it, many of them African Americans. They find characters like Madea and Mr. Brown demeaning caricatures, racial stereotypes.

"Spike Lee has said, and I quote, 'I think there's a lot of stuff out today that is coonery and buffoonery. I see ads for *Meet the Browns* and *House of Payne*, and I'm scratching my head. We've got a black president, and we're going back. The image is troubling, and it harkens back to Amos 'n' Andy.' He's talking about you," Pitts noted.

"I would love to read that to my fan base," Perry said. "Let me tell you what Madea, Brown, all these characters are: bait. Disarming, charming, make-you-laugh bait, so I can slap Madea in something and talk about God, love, faith, forgiveness, family, any of those things, you know. So yes, I think, you know, that pisses me off. It really does."

"It's so insulting," Perry added. "It's attitudes like that that make Hollywood think that these people do not exist. And that's why there's no material speaking to them, speaking to us."

Hilton Als: Tyler Perry Simplifies, Commodifies Black Life

Allison Keyes / 2010

Filmmaker Tyler Perry has made millions from his screen and stage portrayals of the smart-mouth, wise-cracking character Madea. But some argue that Perry's characters and movies demean the black community with harmful stereotypes. *New Yorker* contributing writer Hilton Als talks about his recent piece on this subject.

Allison Keyes: I'm Allison Keyes. This is *Tell Me More* from NPR News. Michel Martin is away.

Coming up, we take a listen to songs from rising Asian American soul singers. That's in a few minutes. But first, she is loud, she's aggressive, she packs heat, and she's no stranger to jail or to church. And when people make her mad, look out. I'm talking about Madea.

(Soundbite of film)

Unidentified Woman: Who are you?
Tyler Perry: (As Madea) Who are you?
Unidentified Woman: I'm the owner of this house.

Perry: Eh, wrong answer. My granddaughter Helen is the owner of this
house. You don't (beep). You ain't got no power or no B.

Unidentified Woman: You can't do this. This is a Vera Wang.

Perry: Who that is? Does she do nails? I need to get my nails did.

Unidentified Woman: That's it. I'm calling the police.

Perry: I ain't scared of no po-po, call the po-po (beep). Call the po-po
(beep).

Keyes: Madea is the brainchild of the highly successful director, writer, and producer, Tyler Perry. In addition to becoming one of the most popular female characters in comedy, Madea has made Perry rich. His films have grossed nearly $450
million domestically. And now, largely thanks to Madea's success, Perry is a major
player in prestigious movie projects.

He joined Oprah to produce the award-winning film *Precious*. And he's currently
producing a film version of the acclaimed play *For Colored Girls Who've Considered
Suicide When the Rainbow Is Enuf*. But Tyler Perry's box office success has earned
him the ire of a vocal band of critics. They chide him as a peddler of simplistic
morality tales that traffic in tired stereotypes of African Americans.

Hilton Als recently wrote about Perry and Madea for *New Yorker* magazine. And
he joins me now from our New York bureau. Welcome to the program.

Hilton Als: Hello.

Keyes: So, in your piece, "Mama's Gun: The World of Tyler Perry," you present him
as an ambitious and determined entrepreneur. But you also kind of throw down
the gauntlet and call Madea, well, an outdated stereotype. Before I ask you why
you think that is, do you think she's funny?

Als: I think she's funny if you were looking at her through a particular lens, which
is to say, as absurdist.

Keyes: Ouch.

Als: I didn't mean to hurt you.

Keyes: Not me personally. I didn't write it. But what do you mean by that?

Als: Well, I think that there is a certain camp element to Madea. There are certain
things about her character that can be amusing, but otherwise I find her to be
grating and annoying.

Keyes: Certain things such as?

Als: If you sort of take a look at her as, how do I say this without getting us all in jail? If you look at her with a critical eye, and if you sort of contextualize her and put her in the tradition of people like Hattie McDaniel and Louise Beavers and, dare I say, a little bit of Whoopi Goldberg in the '80s, you'll see that she really is part of this tradition that has always been a sort of entertainment staple: loudmouth, presumably strong, but slightly ditzy platform, and who's comedy is really based on the fact that she doesn't really know what she's doing half the time.

Keyes: Before we go further with that, though, since you mentioned jail, you know I have to play a clip from *Madea Goes to Jail*, don't you?

Als: I thought it was a good segue myself.

(Soundbite of *Madea Goes to Jail*)

> **Unidentified Man**: Madea.
> **Perry**: Hmm?
> **Unidentified Man:** Now, I know Vanessa wasn't the best girl.
> **Perry:** She was the worst, absolute worse. You couldn't have gotten worse
>   if you had prayed and said, "God, send me worse."

(Soundbite of laughter)

> **Perry:** Blasting me with words (unintelligible).
> **Unidentified Man:** I thought I could change you, Madea.
> **Perry:** You can't change people, son. I don't know what makes folks think
>   they can change somebody. You can't change nobody. That is a waste of
>   time, sitting around trying to change somebody.

(Soundbite of applause)

Perry: Maya Angelou said it best. She said, "If someone shows you who they are, believe them."

Keyes: You were saying slightly ditzy, strong black woman, but there is kind of this stereotypical large, friendly, nurturing black woman that's supposed to kind of keep us all safe from evil in that sort of thing. But that's not who you think this is, is it?

Als: No, if you're just listening to the clip that you played, she's preaching always. It's not a dialogue, and it's not a conversation. So then, therefore, it's not theater or film. It's more of an occasion for sermonizing. That makes her less of a human being than it does an idea—the idea being that someone like Madea is there to tell us how to behave and how to feel.

Keyes: But for all of your issues with her, you've got to admit, she's pretty popular because people are spending bank to go see these movies. What do you think is appealing about her to the audience?

Als: I think that it's largely a sense of security. I don't think that there are many, many strong, black male role models who provide a certain kind of really American, Southern-based comfort that Madea grows out of. She's a signpost in our Obama world of traditional Christian values. And so the comfort that she provides as a figure really has everything to do with the idea of faith being the thing that's going to carry audience members over into Huxtable-like security and sense of self.

Keyes: But why can't people go to the movies—and black people in particular—and see something with a happy ending? Why must it be something, you know, deep and serious and sad?

Als: Because I think that black culture is deep and serious. We can always sort of go to the movies to see various aspects of ourselves. I just don't think that Madea should be the most popular and the touchstone for what blackness means to the cinema.

Keyes: I'm interested that you said that because some people that—I actually was having this conversation with somebody a few days ago, and there are some people that suggest that there aren't other directors that are trying to appeal to communities of color and black people in particular.

Als: Right. Right. Because they don't think that it's an economically feasible market. For instance, it's very, very difficult to get a film made and to presell it to Europe if it has a black female lead because they don't feel that it really sort of translates across or crosses over. I think that Tyler Perry's genius really has been to tap into the domestic market. He knows what his audience is based on having toured America for so long, and then giving them the blueprint for his films prior to the films coming out and then the films have the built-in audience because they've seen it in theaters already.

He has an incredible sense of who his audience is. I'm just saying that why can't there be a different kind of audience taking into consideration a black intellectual audience or a black, you know, various colors, various sexes and ideas?

Keyes: So some people might come back and say, "So why don't you write that."

Als: Well, I've tried, and I can't tell you how daunting it is to take these meetings in Los Angeles and then for them to say this script is brilliant and your casting ideas are brilliant, except that we can't sell it because it's too smart.

Keyes: You think that Hollywood is deliberately allowing films that you don't believe show the huge spectrum of our community because it would cause people to think too hard to watch something else?

Als: You know, it would sort of challenge the idea of what a black audience is, and Tyler Perry has helped institute the idea of the black audience. The idea is that they want a film that really sort of upholds family values, has a sort of Christian basis, and often the conflict has to have a resolution involving being saved by someone with lighter skin.

Keyes: You say in your piece that Madea is the most popular black female comedian on the circuit right now.

Als: Mm-hmm.

Keyes: Which is sort of ironic since she's a man in drag, but that's a whole other issue.

Als: Yeah.

Keyes: But is this because they're not quality roles for black female comedians or that society only has this vision of this one person, this one woman?

Als: Well, I think you touched on something very interesting before, which I had written about, and it's the idea that a lot of black performers don't get work because they're not protected by black or white directors. I think someone like Khandi Alexander, who's now on *Treme*, is one of the most extraordinary actresses I've seen in years. But she's dependent on someone brilliant like David Simon to realize that and to give her a forum. Tyler Perry's not interested in that kind of nuance because it doesn't sell. It's dollars before art in Hollywood.

Keyes: So are you accusing him or Hollywood of exploiting his audience?

Als: I think he's exploiting the preconceptions that Hollywood has about blackness.

Keyes: Hilton Als is a theater critic for the *New Yorker*. He joined us from NPR's New York bureau. Thanks, Hilton for your thoughts.

Als: Thank you so much for having me.

Tyler Perry, Movie Mogul

Sheryl Garratt / 2010

From the *Telegraph*, August 21, 2010. © Telegraph Media Group Limited.
Reprinted by permission.

We are sitting in a plush room in the Dorchester hotel in London, and Tyler Perry, a genial giant of a man whose 6-foot-5-inch frame dwarfs most of the furniture, is saying he would like to kill off an old lady. Not just any old lady, you understand. He is talking about Mabel "Madea" Simmons, a gray-haired matriarch who favors shapeless floral frocks, dishes out advice at full volume whether it is asked for or not, and rules with a tongue as sharp as a samurai's sword—plus occasional help from the gun in her handbag.

Perry created Madea as comic relief in his second play, *I Can Do Bad All by Myself*, in 2000, but since then she has taken on a life of her own on stage, in film, on television, and even in the US bestseller lists with her 2006 book, *Don't Make a Black Woman Take Off Her Earrings*. She is in her late seventies now, and it is hard to imagine what fresh misfortunes could fall on her big, complicated family after all they have been through. But whenever he dares mention retiring her, Perry is deluged with angry letters and emails from her fans. Aretha Franklin wrote to him once: "There are two things that got you to where you are; one is Jesus, the other is Madea. And you'd better not get rid of either one of them!"

Still, it is Perry who has to struggle into the fat-suit and wig every time he plays her. He has the looks of a leading man, and when I wonder if he ever resents dressing up in a frock to go to work, he laughs and says he does, every day. "I resented the fact that she became so famous and so many people loved her because I just didn't get it and I did not get her. But these days grandmothers are much younger, and much busier. Back in the day, there were grandmothers who would be there for you, give you counsel, and I think that's what she represents to a lot of people. Now I'm at a place where as long as the audience loves to see it, I'll do it. But the minute they stop coming, that old broad—she's dead." He roars with laughter. "She's outta here! She is gonna die a quick death."

You may be struggling to place the name, but Tyler Perry is hugely, ridiculously successful. When his plays tour the US, they sell out 15,000-capacity arenas, night after night. The film adaptations—which he writes, directs, and produces—have opening weekends that put many Hollywood blockbusters to shame. In 2008 he opened his own film studios in Atlanta, where five sound stages are kept constantly busy making his movies and his two television series—so much so that he is already planning a $100 million expansion program for it next year. *Forbes* magazine recently placed him at number six in its chart of Hollywood's biggest earners. Yet his work is only just about to be released here on DVD, and next month his ninth film, *Why Did I Get Married Too?*, will be the first to show in British cinemas. Even in the US, he says, it is only recently that the major players in the film industry began taking his calls.

Perry has built his success by creating family entertainment with a Christian message that deals with the challenges, hopes, and aspirations of the silent majority of African Americans whose lives are not reflected in the aggression of hip-hop, no matter how real the rappers say they are keeping their lyrics. Perry's plots are pure melodrama with more twists and turns than a Turkey Twizzler, usually centered on a wronged woman who is finally rewarded with the love of a humble but good man, with music, laughter, and often some politically incorrect interjections from Madea along the way. He hones the plays on the road, where he ad-libs constantly on stage and the audiences' very vocal responses let him know exactly what they like and what they don't.

Critics say that he deals in stereotypes, that his messages are too preachy and simplistic, and that there is not a social problem, from crack addiction to unemployment, that cannot be cured in his world by love, faith, and the power of prayer. There may be truth in this, but Perry is unashamedly populist and, above all, when his name is above the title, his audience knows it will be entertained, and that it is something all the family can safely see.

Now forty-one, Perry grew up in New Orleans, a city few of us really knew until Hurricane Katrina exposed the reality behind its pretty facades. "There are these big beautiful mansions that line the streets," he says, "but two blocks behind them there's complete and utter poverty."

Perry's father, Emmitt Perry Sr., had an upbringing that was tougher than most. (Perry was also given the name Emmitt but changed it to Tyler at the age of sixteen to dissociate himself from his father.) Abandoned by his natural parents as a toddler, Emmitt Sr. was found in a drainage canal in Louisiana and given to a fourteen-year-old farm girl to raise. "She was two generations out of slavery," Perry explains quietly. "So anything that he would do wrong, she would beat him. She beat him and beat him and beat him. So I came along and I'm the first boy, and anything I did wrong, he would beat me. He hated my guts."

Perry's skin was darker than his father's, making Emmitt doubt that he was really his child. He also suffered from asthma. "He was angry that I was always ill and I couldn't work. To him, men were strong. I'd be reading a book, and he would knock it out of my hand: 'What are you reading for? That's not going to get you anywhere—you have to work!' We were just polar opposites."

To protect her only son, his mother would take him with her wherever she went. "I'd be in the beauty salon, playing with my Matchbox cars, listening to all these women talk. Then watching her pain and the pain of my three sisters, and being the only boy in that situation, it just gave me a sensitivity to women. Often, when I'm writing those characters, I'm thinking of my mother, and her voice."

By the time he was seventeen, he was "numb with anger," but he was also bigger than his father, so the beatings stopped. Four years later, he went on a trip to Atlanta, Georgia, the prosperous capital of the South, and finally found somewhere he felt he belonged. "For the first time, I saw African American people doing well, who spoke well, who had careers and were successful and went out to dinner with their families—things I had never done, never experienced. I knew I was home. And I knew my life would change there."

His mother, Willie Maxine, died last year, and stayed with her husband until the end. Things were different for her generation, Tyler says, but he takes great pride in the fact that fans have been inspired by his work to walk away from abusive relationships. It is also why he came on board as an executive producer of *Precious*, the harrowing but life-affirming film about parental abuse that won a best supporting actress Oscar for Mo'Nique, who played the monstrous mother. "When I first saw it I sat in the screening-room for a bit afterwards, gathering myself, because somebody had written my story," he says. "The female character played by Mo'Nique—that is my father, to this day."

Yet when he talks about his childhood now, it is without a trace of bitterness. It is what shaped him. "I didn't want to be the kind of man that my father was. So I've tried, my entire life, to be the complete and utter opposite of that. And it has served not only the art well, but I think the audience well."

It was Oprah Winfrey—now a friend and his partner in bringing *Precious* to a wider audience—who started him writing, soon after he moved to Atlanta. On her television show one day she talked about how cathartic it can be to write things down. He was watching the show, and once he had bought a dictionary—"I went to a very substandard school, so I didn't even know what 'cathartic' meant"—he began writing about the abuse he had experienced, hiding behind characters in case anyone realized what he had been through. Eventually he shaped it into a play about adult survivors of abuse, *I Know I've Been Changed*.

Having saved up money from a variety of low-paid jobs, in 1992 he hired a small theater to put it on, hoping to attract an audience of 1,200 over the short run. He sold only thirty tickets. Perry now feels there was something he needed to do first: make his peace with his father.

"I had to forgive him," he says simply. "I was so angry and bitter and so full of hate and frustration, and I did not want to be that way anymore. He and I had an argument, and I said some things that I'd never said before. And something changed inside of me." Afterwards, Perry got help, turned to his faith to strengthen him, and began the long journey to understanding. He is now reconciled with his father. "It's not an easy journey, to get to a place where you forgive people. But it is such a powerful place, because it frees you."

In 1998 he tried again with the play. The script hadn't changed much, he says, but this time there was sincerity in its message of forgiveness and redemption. Crucially, he also added music, recruiting singers from local churches to perform it, and he toured those churches to talk about the play. This brought in an audience, who liked what they saw and told their friends—suddenly, he had a hit.

He began to tour the so-called Chitlin Circuit, the kind of small venues in black areas where stars such as Billie Holiday and Sam Cooke established their reputations during segregation. As the word spread, the venues got bigger, as did Perry's fortune. But he worked hard for it, putting on 200–300 shows, with at least one new play, a year. As another income stream, he also began filming the performances and selling the DVDs. The piracy rate was fierce, he laughs, but it helped spread the word, and in five years his mailing list grew to more than a million names.

When he went to the studios with the idea of making a film out of one of his plays, *Diary of a Mad Black Woman*, the response was lukewarm. The middle-aged, church-going black women who formed the core of his loyal audience didn't go to the cinema, he was told, and the melodramatic script—in which a married woman is pushed out of her palatial home so her lawyer husband can move in his mistress, but eventually finds the love of a hard-working man who doesn't want sex before marriage—would need major changes. So instead he formed a partnership with an independent distributor, Lionsgate, which puts up half the production costs for his films and takes half the profits, while letting Perry control and ultimately own the content. It is an unusual deal, but one that has worked well. With little or no advertising—he simply sent out an email to his mailing list and let word of mouth do the rest—in 2005 *Diary* took more than $50 million at the US box office, then sold 2.5 million copies on DVD in its first week. It had cost only $5.5 million to make. "We've done a billion dollars of business in five years," Perry says matter-of-factly. "So it's been a great partnership."

When he decided to branch out into TV in 2007, he cut a similarly canny deal. He made the first ten episodes of Tyler Perry's *House of Payne* at his studios and offered it to the TV networks to show for nothing, alerting his mailing list when it was due to be screened. Thanks to his mailing list again, it drew record-breaking viewing figures, so they ordered twenty-four more. For most sitcoms, this would be a considerable success, but Perry said he wanted a bigger commitment, and eventually secured an order for a hundred episodes. "That has never been heard of in the history of television. It takes a week to do a sitcom in Hollywood. I do a show a day in my studio, three or four shows a week. So what takes most shows eight years to do, we do in a year."

House of Payne—about three generations of a working-class African American family living in the same home—has run continually since, and Perry has launched a second successful series, a spin-off from his film *Meet the Browns*. The rewards have been great. He built a vast mansion just outside Atlanta, outgrew it, and built a bigger one closer to town. He has homes in Los Angeles and New York, owns a small island in the Bahamas—"that's my hideaway, my little piece of heaven"— and has his own jet to travel between all these places. But he squirms when I ask about this. He is similarly reluctant to discuss the woman in his life, saying only that she works in New York and lives in his apartment there, and that children are definitely on the agenda.

Despite his wealth, he has never lost touch with the needs of his audience. Aware that not all of them have bank accounts, let alone credit cards, he always gives them the option of paying by money order. Because big chains such as Blockbuster are rarely found in poorer neighborhoods, he approached small shops in black areas to rent out his DVDs. After every performance of his plays, he comes on stage to chat to the audience, tell them what he is up to next, and play them a trailer of the next film or TV show.

"Those audiences are my critics," he says. "They tell me right away! I learnt very early on how far I can go, what I can and can't say on stage. They inspire the stories that I tell, and how I tell them. It has to be something that the core can relate to. And what I'm finding is that if you serve the core, it grows, and you find a whole new audience."

His schedule is still relentless. He wrote and directed the first hundred episodes of the sitcoms himself, to establish their style. This year, he toured with a new play, *Madea's Big Happy Family*, performing 125 shows in 126 days. Over the summer he will make this into a film, before going back on the road with the play for another three months. He will also film his adaptation of the poet Ntozake Shange's 1975 play *For Colored Girls Who Have Considered Suicide When the Rainbow Is Enuf*.

"I don't sleep very much," he smiles, when I ask how he does it. "And I have a good team around me." On the plane to London, he sketched out a pilot for a new sitcom. On the way back, he planned to write another. Even while we are talking, he jokes, he is working. "I'm writing a movie now. You just don't know it."

His friend, the singer Janet Jackson, says this is not far from the truth: 'We talk a lot, and we've become pretty good friends. But only three times have I ever known him to take some time off. And never for long periods. He's a workaholic, and he likes to multitask. He's taught me that you've got to have several things going on at once."

Jackson met him after going to see one of the plays, and shortly after received a script for *Why Did I Get Married?*, a film about a group of professional couples who go on holiday at a ski resort. Jackson plays a psychologist who is good at solving the problems for everyone else, while constantly suppressing her own feelings. It is a role she reprises in *Why Did I Get Married Too?*, in which the same group meet for a holiday in the Caribbean a few years later and tussle with problems from unemployment to infidelity and domestic violence.

The news of her brother Michael's death came just as Jackson was preparing to leave New York to start filming. Perry says he offered to postpone the shoot, but she wanted to work. There is a scene where her character destroys her living room with her husband's golf clubs. It was, she says, a release. "It was very therapeutic. I needed it. We did three takes, and I broke three golf clubs! There was a lot stuffed up inside, but I enjoyed being able to vent."

Jackson wrote the theme tune for the film and will also be starring in *For Colored Girls*, alongside Mariah Carey, Whoopi Goldberg, and the *Cosby Show* star Phylicia Rashad. But despite increasingly starry casts, Perry still keeps the budget of each of his films below $20 million, usually shooting in less than two months.

Tyler Perry's Hollywood:
Diary of a Mad Black . . . Mogul

Roger Brooks / 2011

From Success.com, September 5, 2011. Reprinted by permission.

Success is a slippery word. Ask a dozen people to define it, and you'll receive twelve different answers, none of them wrong. Take a poll on how to find it, and hundreds of paths will suddenly appear amongst the trees. The right trail is always changing, multiplying, and contracting—different for each of us. See? Slippery.

So how would you define success for a poor black boy growing up in 1970s New Orleans? Would you lower expectations if you knew his father was so abusive he once attempted suicide to escape the beatings? If you knew he was molested by several different people in his community, would that alter how you judged his progress through life? For this boy, success might simply mean surviving childhood. Maybe, if he's lucky, he'll find the path that leads to being a kind man with a decent job. Nothing special.

"Nothing special" is not good enough for Tyler Perry. The little boy from New Orleans not only survived, he became the most unlikely power broker in Hollywood, earning millions and connecting with a legion of fans with his poignant, funny, down-to-earth interpretations of African American family life in his plays, movies, and sitcoms. Perry took his own route to success, if only because the easiest paths were blocked by his turbulent childhood. But his upbringing also gave him the tools he needed to hack through the trees and underbrush as he blazed his own trail.

"You have to understand everything that has happened to you, especially things beyond your control, weren't about trying to destroy you as much as they were about molding and forming you as a person," says the creator of *Diary of a Mad Black Woman*, the Madea series and Tyler Perry's *House of Payne*. "That's really difficult for a lot of people to understand. But if you begin to realize every moment in your life happened for the greater good of who you are, you can use it for others. It can really elevate you and change your whole trajectory. I think that's what happened to me."

THIS TOO SHALL PASS

Perry's experiences were enough to break most people. The pain and anger grew inside him like a fire, eating away at him. It wasn't until he caught an episode of *The Oprah Winfrey Show* championing the therapeutic benefits of journaling that Perry's outlook began to change. But even on the private pages of his diary, he couldn't be truly honest about his tragic upbringing. Fearful others might read his words, he invented characters who revealed his experiences and feelings. In the process, he let the hate and venom flow through his pen. He was still livid, but he had a place to siphon off the bile when it threatened to overwhelm him.

"Journaling gets it out of you and on to paper; it is a catharsis," Perry says. "It helps you to understand, unload, and heal. And what is amazing about it, if you go back to something you'd written a year ago—be it fear, struggles, something you couldn't get past—when I went back and looked through all the things I thought were huge for me to get past, being able to read [about them] inspires me. It encourages me that everything is OK; this too shall pass."

But it wasn't until a friend found his diary that something clicked.

"Man, Tyler, this is a really good play."

Suddenly, Perry looked at his words in a new light and a different kind of fire settled in his stomach. He left New Orleans for Atlanta—not exactly a hotbed of performance art, but Perry's path to success is not one well-traveled.

"I knew I wouldn't be in a position to come to Hollywood and audition and act and all those things; I had to have another way," Perry recalls. "I knew more of what I didn't want to do than what I did want to do. . . . I couldn't imagine going to LA. It's such a tough road for people. I have such a respect for people who can come into this town and get into this system and strive and be successful. It drains me; it rips at the very fabric of my soul to do that. I wanted to come in my own way, and the plays seemed the best entrance."

WHY DOES THIS MAKE ME ANGRY?

Perry didn't find instant success in Atlanta either—far from it. He took jobs as a bill collector, a hotel housekeeper, and a used car salesman, among others. He sometimes lived out of his car to make ends meet. *I Know I've Been Changed* debuted in 1992, costing him his life savings of $12,000 to produce. It was widely panned and sparsely attended before quickly closing. Over the next six years, Perry constantly tweaked the play, tightening the action and revealing his themes of self-respect and redemption more clearly. By 1998, Perry was so discouraged by his constant failings that he was ready to give up.

"I was losing faith. In those six years of struggling, I'd really gotten to a point of thinking this is never going to work," Perry remembers. "But every time I thought that, there was someone else who'd come along and help my dream find a new life."

Perry tried one last time. On opening night, even as he was deciding it was time to give up his dream, people lined up outside the theater. The show played to packed houses and rave reviews. He took his play on the road, created new productions, and perfected his signature style of portraying everyday African American families featuring strong women, lots of laughs, and the sometimes-ugly realities that go on behind closed doors.

"The great thing about writing is that every character has a motivation," Perry says. "When I started to track down characters' motivations, I started to do the same thing to my own motivations. Why does this bother me so much? Why does that make me angry? So once I tracked down motivations back to the root, it allowed me to untie a lot of the anger and release the sting."

The root, Perry found, was his father. Shortly before he played to sold-out shows in 1998, he called his dad to tell him the harm he had caused, the anger he had hatched inside his son. Instead of fighting back, his father said only, "I love you," before hanging up the phone. Perry knew immediately something was different.

WRITING WHAT HE KNOWS

"I knew something had changed, but I didn't know that I had just gone from a diesel engine to unleaded, and the fuel I had used—anger—wouldn't burn anymore. It wouldn't motivate or inspire me," Perry says. "I had to find a new way to use everything else I had in me to keep going. That became the opposite energy of negativity—positivity. This is what happened to me. This is what I went through. How do I pass this on to inspire and encourage someone else?"

Perry was reaching hundreds of thousands of people across the South with his plays, but to get his message out to the masses he'd have to tackle Hollywood. In 2005, the film adaptation of *Diary of a Mad Black Woman* was released. It grossed more than $50 million, ten times what it cost to produce the movie. The project was a success monetarily, but it also laid the groundwork for Perry's popularity. Audiences fell in love with the grumpy, tell-it-like-it-is, tough-loving grandmother Madea, played by Perry himself. A fan favorite from Perry's plays, the character became the focal point of three films, but has appeared in six of the ten movies Perry has starred in. She also appears in the TBS series Tyler Perry's *House of Payne*.

Some have criticized Perry, saying his characters invoke racial stereotypes that demean African Americans. Spike Lee reportedly described Perry's work as "coonery and buffoonery." When reading the quote during a 2009 interview with Byron Pitts for CBS's *60 Minutes*, Perry said, "That pisses me off. It's attitudes like that that make Hollywood think these people don't exist, and that's why there's no material speaking to them—speaking to us."

Perry says Madea combines elements of the strong women of his childhood. "I don't know if any culture is like the black culture when it comes to the woman," he says. "[The woman] is at times the mother and father, she is the strength, the love, and the corrector. That is the way it was in my house. My mother was a major role model. Just her care and love for people and how she took care of all of us. How her heart only beat one way; she only knew love."

DO ONE THING WELL

Now Perry, forty-two, is among the Hollywood elite, ranked No. 19 on *Forbes'* Celebrity 100 List of most powerful people in entertainment, and No. 3 on the list based on his earnings, estimated at $130 million (behind U2 and Oprah Winfrey). His movies make money, and he captures the attention of the African American demographic like no one else.

But old habits die hard, and Perry hasn't let go of the person who made him a success. Angry and introverted as a young man, Perry still has trust issues. He works at least fourteen hours a day, oversees almost every aspect of his projects, and remains single. There's no one to tell him to stop, slow down, or share the burden—a fact Perry seems to revel in. It's a system that works for him; he's not used to taking the well-traveled path to success. He remains wary of Hollywood, going so far as to build his own state-of-the-art studio in Atlanta so he can remain close to home.

Convention aside, Perry believes the secret to his career is simple, something anyone can apply to their own pursuits. For "someone who is trying to be success-ful—who has an idea and doesn't know if it will happen or work—you have to find one thing," Perry says. "I know people are jacks-of-all-trades and do a million things but find one thing and do it so well that it affords you the opportunity to do all the other things."

And Perry, like anyone else, has his own definition of success, his own opinion on the right path to choose to cross the dark, intimidating forest.

"Success for me has clearly been about being able to live in the present—live fully and in this moment," Perry says. "Learning how to come down into the mo-ment and really appreciate it and enjoy it, that's what success is. When you can do that, every moment of your life will be successful. Whatever you're working on, whatever your business, whatever you're trying to be, if you can be fully in the moment, I think that will change your life."

You don't need to work Tyler Perry's long hours to maximize your productivity the way he does.

Tyler Perry is an admitted workaholic. He'll focus on a project until he is exhausted, searching for what he calls a "workman's high," similar to the runner's high many elite athletes enjoy. It's a habit Perry doesn't recommend you pick up. "Working that hard that much and not taking care of yourself can be a weakness," he says. "I enjoy it, but I'll push past a point where I know I should stop."

But you don't have to work like Perry to learn from his habits. Here are a few of his strategies for squeezing the most out of every minute.

* Keep thinking. Perry starts his morning at 5:30 a.m. by working out. While exercising, he thinks about his upcoming day—what needs to be accomplished, what problems he's likely to face, and what solutions he'll need to develop. His multitasking allows him to get the physical activity he needs while still being productive.

* Take time out. During the middle of his day, Perry takes time to be alone in his office. Perry is a big believer in listening to his inner voice, which he says can be hard to hear during the cacophony of the day. "I call it my God voice. I listen to God through that voice. It's difficult to hear sometimes when things are so crowded and busy. I have to make sure I center myself, especially when I need clarity or answers about the next thing I'm supposed to do. . . . Emotion aside, just get in a clear, quiet place and see how I feel about it. If it feels right, I'll move forward. And every time I've gone against that I've ended up in a bad situation."

* Always be searching. Perry has a journal app on his phone so he can record inspiration wherever he sees it. That way, even when he's not working, his brain is engaged and open to good ideas.

* Be in the moment. Everyone works hard—it's the price of being successful—but Perry encourages you to enjoy a job well done. "Learning how to come down into the moment and really appreciate it and enjoy it," he says, "that's what success is."

Tyler Perry Interview: "I Want My Films to Be Relevant to People's Lives"

Samantha Ofole-Prince / 2014

From Gospelherald.com, March 11, 2014. Reprinted by permission.

There's a familiar thread that runs through most of Tyler Perry's films, for the actor, director, and playwright has long embraced religion in his projects.

Whether it's *Good Deeds*, *Why Did I Get Married?*, *The Family That Preys*, or his latest film *The Single Moms Club*, there's always a life-affirming message about faith, family, and friendship.

"Being a man of faith, I don't want to do films just to make money," shares Perry, who was born into poverty and raised in a household scarred by abuse. "If it's not speaking to somebody or not encouraging somebody, then I am not doing what I am here to do. There are lots of people who do film and television and entertain, but I feel like I have a responsibility to impact some sort of something."

Sharing meaningful and uplifting stories is Perry's top priority. In eight years, he's helmed several inspirational-themed films and plays including *Woman Thou Art Loosed*, a collaboration with pastor T. D. Jakes, and fought from a young age to find the strength, faith, and perseverance that would later form the foundations of his much-acclaimed projects.

Physically abused by his father and sexually molested by other adults, he's been able to transcend his horrific childhood by writing stories and is the first African American to own a major film and TV studio.

His first play *I Know I've Been Changed*, which he spent his life savings to produce in 1992 was a gospel musical about two adult survivors of child abuse. With just a handful of people in the audience, the play was a flop, and he spent several years living in his car and credits his faith in God for sustaining him through the dark years.

His core audiences are black churchgoers, but Perry has managed through a distribution deal with Lionsgate studio and collaboration with the Oprah Winfrey

Network (OWN) to tap into mainstream America. His films, plays, and the TV shows on the cable networks TBS and OWN have featured several award-winning actors and actresses from *Cosby Show*'s Keshia Knight Pulliam, Louis Gossett Jr., Janet Jackson, Angela Bassett, Kathy Bates, and Kerry Washington to Wendi McLendon-Covey, who stars in his latest film, *The Single Moms Club*.

A film which follows a group of single mothers who create a support group, for Perry, who is taking a break from film to concentrate on TV, it's a project that's long overdue.

"This movie is something I needed to be addressed and is something I have wanted to do for a while, as I felt that it would be inspiring and really encouraging to a lot of people. This is about women who are doing what they have to do for their kids and making it happen."

Also starring Nia Long, Amy Smart, Cocoa Brown, Terry Crews, and William Levy, Perry's spirited comedy follows five single mothers whose children—thanks to a generous scholarship program—all attend an exclusive prep school. The mothers range from a white career-driven woman to an African American fast food worker who find themselves united after their children are threatened with expulsion for bad behavior. Together, they form the Single Moms Club, a haven for single mothers seeking support and an understanding ear.

"What was important for me to show is that no matter what your background or color is we are all dealing with the same issues. We are all in the same situation and all need support for each other," adds the media mogul who hopes the Single Moms Club model might inspire other single mothers to form clubs of their own. "I want my films to be relevant to people's lives and give them hope, so it's important to deal with subjects like single parenthood and poverty, but at the same time point the way forward through laughter, love, and faith."

Tyler Perry Shares His Life's Lessons

Eric Peterson / 2014

From the *Daily Herald*, August 16, 2014. Reprinted by permission of Jim Baumann, Managing Editor, the *Daily Herald*.

Faith in God and a desire to champion underdogs like himself took Tyler Perry from a poor and abusive household in Louisiana to being one of the most influential voices in American entertainment.

The actor, filmmaker, writer, and director spoke about the life lessons he's both learned and taught during Willow Creek Community Church's Global Leadership Summit in South Barrington Friday.

In front of a packed church, Willow Creek Senior Pastor Bill Hybels interviewed Perry about the many dualities of his life—poverty and affluence, artist and businessman, anger and forgiveness.

Perry said the creative and business roles he juggles in his life are ones he tries to keep rigidly separated for both their sakes. But he believes both are products of the pain and joy he experienced in childhood.

"For me, they were both born in the same place," Perry said. "They're like twins in my head."

His alcoholic and abusive father created in him a need to escape through imagination. But his father's work ethic and pride as a carpenter and contractor were an equal influence, he said.

Perry finds both traits necessary not only in his own work but also in those he works with. He finds it difficult to interact with people whose artistic gifts have crowded out all self-discipline and business sense.

But when hiring people at his thirty-acre studio campus near Atlanta, he's more likely to go with the person less qualified on paper but who possesses the right attitude.

"What I try to do is surround myself with people that are like me," Perry said. "I was the underdog."

Perry spoke about the long, difficult relationship he had with his abusive father and the path to glory that was shown to him by his mother.

"Being a little boy there, not being able to protect her, was traumatic to me," Perry said.

But every Sunday morning his mother would wake him up to take him to church, where he would see this victimized woman transformed into a singing, dancing, joyful person.

"I want to know the God that makes my mother so happy," he thought. "I want to know that Jesus."

Hybels commended Perry for addressing in his writings an aspect of forgiveness too often overlooked by most Christian theologians. Though it's expected and beneficial, it's far from easy.

Perry said it takes as much energy to forgive someone who has wronged you as it did to survive their abuse or betrayal in the first place.

"You can't just turn on a switch and it goes away!" he said.

What was scary to him about forgiving his father was having to give up the fuel that had sustained his quest for success up to that point. But freeing oneself from the effects of another's bad influence provides its own reward, he said.

"You do not deserve that, and they do not deserve to have that kind of power over you," Perry said.

In talking about Perry's work itself, Hybels could hardly avoid the recurring character of the wise but crusty Madea, whom Perry has played in several films.

Perry said the original influence came from seeing Eddie Murphy play an older woman in *The Nutty Professor* films. But Madea herself is specifically "a PG version" of the women in his own family. Many of her mannerisms come from one particular aunt, while Perry's mother is the kind side of the character, he explained.

In all of his television series, films, and plays, Perry said he wants there to be a message, not just a story or a laugh. One much more serious film, *Good Deeds*, reflected his own experiences of being both a "have" and a "have not," and how people from those two worlds relate to each other.

Dealing with critics is a responsibility shared by both the artist and the leader, Perry said. When two critics once varyingly described one of his plays as both the best and worst thing they'd ever seen, he realized critics are more often describing their own life experiences than the work of art itself.

He was once told that a woman who'd planned to commit suicide gathered her kids together for what—unknown to them—she intended to be their final weekend of fun together. One child asked that they watch a Tyler Perry play on DVD, which ended up inspiring the mother with a new perspective on her life.

No bad review could compete with the importance of that, he said.

Asked to comment about the state of race relations in the US—especially with tensions boiling in Ferguson, Missouri, over the fatal shooting of an unarmed teen by a police officer—Perry said gradual improvement is all one can expect.

"What I hope is that every generation gets better, and I think that's what's happening," he said. "It's not going to happen overnight."

On philanthropy, Perry said at first he simply felt so guilty about having money that he gave it all away. But once that passed, he became more thoughtful and strategic about identifying needs and where money could do the most good. "I'm my mother's son, and she had a heart for giving," Perry said.

The Brand Keeping Oprah in Business

Rembert Browne / 2015

From *New York* magazine, December 28, 2015. Reprinted by permission of Rembert Browne/*New York* magazine.

"Really? Tyler Perry? I couldn't stand *Think Like a Man*."

I should have corrected her, but my bartender at this hookah bar in downtown Atlanta had already turned around to fix another drink. It might have been the perfect reaction to my telling a stranger—and a black woman, at that—that I had just spent the afternoon with Perry. She was not only confused and borderline upset that I had done such a thing, she was blaming him for a movie she hated—one he didn't even make.

As a brand name, Tyler Perry is recognizable. He's gotten extremely rich producing movies, TV shows, and stage plays featuring predominantly black casts and Christian themes that are about as subtle as trumpet fanfare. In some parts of the country, Perry might go unrecognized, and in others he's well known but dismissed. For years Perry's been maligned, and Spike Lee famously described his work as "coonery" a few years back, fueling a complicated debate about race, class, and the duty of black storytellers to their community.

Just a week earlier, in Flatbush, Brooklyn, though, Perry was unconditionally appreciated. The enthusiastic Sunday afternoon line at the Kings Theatre post-church performance of *Madea on the Run*—Perry's twentieth touring stage play in twenty-three years—went down the block and around the corner. It was one of seven sold-out performances in a four-day stretch, and the audience was as old, black, and female as I would have imagined. I'd watched a few of these plays on tape at family gatherings over the years, so I could guess that the group in line was probably more Christian than not, with a taste for gospel, laughter, and some overarching moral conclusion, told through the accessible lens of a family drama. And I knew they preferred to be entertained by black people, specifically Perry.

I did not expect to enjoy this show. This was Tyler Perry, after all, and I'm a professional cultural critic. But after a few minutes, I slipped up and laughed. Then

Perry—playing Madea, an old-lady character with a penchant for skipping church and smoking weed but then schooling "good Christians" who aren't actually as pious as they seem—forgot a line and said, "I'll remember it, I wrote the thing." Right there, I really laughed.

During the curtain call, Tyler Perry walked out last, dressed as himself—jeans, a shirt, a black fitted cap. "You guys have always been so faithful to me," he said to the crowd, which was still in the middle of a standing ovation. "Always right there by my side, always supporting me, even when it wasn't that great." He then broke into an old-lady voice that wasn't quite the Madea old-lady voice, close to the voice of the old lady two seats down. *"Bless his heart, he'll get better."* He thanked them for watching his four television shows currently on OWN (the Oprah Winfrey Network), especially the breakout hit *The Haves and the Have Nots*, the network's highest-rated show ever, which will return January 5. The season-three finale pulled in 3.71 million viewers, making it the third-highest scripted cable telecast of the summer, only behind episodes of *Pretty Little Liars* and *Fear the Walking Dead*. "Let's face it, there's no need for me to go out there [onstage] anymore," Perry would tell me later. "The only reason is to be in front of them and to tell them how much I appreciate them, make them laugh, see their faces—and it does a great thing for me and my heart, too. It just gets me reconnected." There's an argument to be made that these days, Perry is largely responsible for keeping the Oprah endeavor relevant, and with shows I'd only just learned existed. But that's how Perry has always operated: success in plain sight.

Perry was born in New Orleans to an abusive father and a mother who taught preschool. While he was estranged from his father—at sixteen, he changed his first name from Emmitt to Tyler so as not to be his father's namesake—he loved his mother. "He worshipped the ground she walked on," said Cicely Tyson, a frequent collaborator who met Perry's mother before she died in 2009. "Took care of her like she was his child." Perry grew up very poor. "My family never went to a restaurant together; we never went to the movies together. Vacation, we never did that," he said as we pulled out of his film studios, nestled in the predominantly black Greenbriar neighborhood of Atlanta—locally famous for its mall, flea market, and a shop dedicated to gold teeth. It was just the two of us in his Porsche Cayenne, weaving through the streets of the city that he's called home since the early 1990s. Like many black college-age adults of the '80s and early '90s—even those who, like him, didn't go to college—Perry first made his way to Atlanta for Freaknik, the unofficial black spring-break extravaganza. But what drew him into the city more permanently wasn't the parties, he said, but the black businessmen and women, a type he'd never seen in real life. "It was the promised land, I tell you. And I dreamed here like never before."

I was reminded of that sentiment, both spiritual and aspirational, by what I saw when I entered Tyler Perry Studios earlier that morning. The phrase "A Place Where Even Dreams Believe" was emblazoned across the glass doors of the lobby. A cluster of stained-glass windows greeted you upon walking through the glass doors. And as you got closer to his office, the walls increasingly filled with massive photos that told the history of black Hollywood, from Josephine Baker to Will Smith. It's clear that Tyler Perry sees himself as part of a lineage, that his present-day storytelling continues the work of those he claimed as his ancestors.

With Hartsfield-Jackson Airport in the background, we pulled up to Perry's first apartment building in Atlanta, a complex that's equal parts subdivision and housing project. While he lived here in his early twenties, his commute included a five-mile walk to the train, which would then take him to the bus, which would then take him to his job as a bill collector on the north side of town—at least, until he was evicted for being unable to pay his own bills. "I was devastated when I came home, and all my things were out on the street, in the rain," he said. "I didn't have much, but the thing I was most upset about was my stereo." But despite the setbacks, it was in this apartment that Perry began his creative exploration. After watching an episode of *The Oprah Winfrey Show* that focused on the therapeutic powers of writing, he began keeping a diary, writing entries that would become his first play. In 1992, the self-funded *I Know I've Been Changed*—a gospel musical about adult characters still dealing with childhood abuse and how God helped them overcome their struggles—made its way to the stage. It was not well received. But he continued to work on the play for the next six years, finally finding success in a local theater in 1998. Things happened quickly after that: a two-year national tour, another play, and then another one after that, 2001's *Diary of a Mad Black Woman*, which would become the inspiration, four years later, for Perry's first film, starring Perry himself as Madea.

The movie version of *Diary of a Mad Black Woman* was widely panned by critics. Roger Ebert ended his review with, "I've been reviewing movies for a long time, and I can't think of one that more dramatically shoots itself in the foot." The *New York Times*' Stephen Holden described it as "soap opera to slapstick to church sermon and back," and "Cinderella meets *Amos 'n' Andy* in Sunday school." It didn't matter. Perry was already a phenomenon, having earned tens of millions of dollars from his plays, and the movie opened at No. 1 at the box office, grossing $21.9 million in its first weekend. Fifteen hugely profitable films would follow, as well as six television shows, most of which had Perry's name in the title, just so you never forgot who was behind the empire. He was not only successful but groundbreaking, too, creating roles that did not exist anywhere else on the same scale for black and other minority actors. "Let's go down the list," Perry said to me confidently. "Idris Elba, first movie. Sofía Vergara. Taraji. Kerry Washington. Viola Davis. I honestly don't know if I had anything to do with that success; all I'm saying is that they all stopped by on their way to wherever they were going." As years passed, he became so important to the local economy that the current mayor of Atlanta, Kasim Reed, personally persuaded him to keep his studios in the city instead of moving them to the suburbs—which resulted in Perry purchasing a large portion of a decommissioned Army base, Fort McPherson. He was also a man who amassed such a fortune that he could afford to purchase a portion of a decommissioned Army base.

Perry's financial success is near impossible to comprehend—unless you're his inspiration-turned-friend-and-colleague, Oprah Winfrey. "This just happened last week—it had never happened before," she told me on the phone. (The list of people for whom Oprah will talk to reporters: probably short.) "So he was at Teterboro Airport, leaving, and I was coming. And our planes pulled up next to each other. And we just had this howling moment, like, 'How in the world did this happen to us?' And we have this 'my jet or yours' moment. Both he and I are these little black kids who came from nowhere and now get to live this amazing life. And we are in full awe of it, all the time, and it never becomes something that you take for granted."

This is simultaneously the least and most relatable story I've ever heard. It's a billionaire telling a tale about a chance encounter with the private jet of her near-billionaire friend. On the surface, there's not much there to identify with. But when you consider the true rags-to-riches story that is their lives—both rags and riches to extremes that the average person could not fathom—the story registers. And that vacillation between absurdity and commonality, that ability to identify with the rags while living among the riches, is the foundation of Perry's empire.

To Perry, though, it seemed as though the more powerful he got, the more his career was undermined. His fans could never shout their reasons for liking Tyler Perry at the same volume as those who thought his material was bad—and many of the most vocal critics are themselves black, angry at what Perry is peddling, the characters they see as caricature, the narratives his stories reinforce. In the same 2009 interview in which Spike Lee referred to Perry's work as "coonery," Lee said, "I see these two ads for these two shows [*Tyler Perry's Meet the Browns* and *House of Payne*], and I am scratching my head. We got a black president, and we going back to Mantan Moreland and Sleep n' Eat?"

"That 'coonery' buffoonery was a direct Spike Lee quote," Perry told me. "And that's what everybody started to say, with those words in particular. But you have to be careful, because our audiences cross-pollinate a lot of times. There's a lot of my audience that likes what he does. And there's a lot of his audience that likes what I do. And when you make those kinds of broad, general strokes, and you paint your audiences in them, they go, 'Wait a minute, are you talking about me? Are you talking about my mom?'"

Perry has often ignored his critics. (Though he did once tell Lee to "kiss my ass.") Perhaps because it doesn't seem to affect his profits, it genuinely doesn't bother him. But chances are it does. Chances are it cuts deep. Because most of the criticisms aren't about his business sense, his ability to direct, or his acting chops—typically, they're about him as a net loss for the black race.

Perry lives in a seventeen-acre compound in the wealthy, very white West Paces Ferry neighborhood. The former owner of the land was a longtime segregationist: Moreton Rolleston, the owner of the downtown Heart of Atlanta motel who was so against integrating his establishment that he took his gripe to the Supreme Court. (He lost.) A neighbor once told Perry that Rolleston stated in the deed of the home, "You cannot sell to niggers." Waiting for the gate to his home to open, Perry finished his story about Rolleston, saying, "To have this property was such poetic justice." He clearly derives joy from being in places and spaces in which he was never supposed to be allowed. And in those spaces, his focus on his lineage and his past only intensifies. "I told this story at a party I was having, and Congressman John Lewis was in the back listening to it," he said. "After the party, he walked up to me in tears and said, 'I was one of the young men that sat in at his lunch counter trying to integrate. And here I am, dancing on the property that he once owned.'"

I was suddenly hit with the reality that I would need to be honest with Perry. I knew I had been wrong about him, to some degree, and I wanted him to know that. But I'd also have to tell him that I spent years disliking him and his work, thinking his characters were negatively affecting me as a black person in a white world. That I knew black people were often judged by what people saw or heard, more than what they knew. That I felt black people were often collectively judged by their perceived failures instead of their perceived successes—the latter of which have long been treated as exceptions. That I knew research existed that analyzed the complicated relationships black people have with the images we see of ourselves on the screen, telling us that those images can inspire, but they can also cause great anxiety. That some black people took black characters merely as "entertainment," but others saw them as images that they needed to instill racial pride, strengthen racial identity, counter racism, and be role models.

A decade of thoughts about Tyler Perry ran through my mind in that moment, and even if he'd made me laugh in Brooklyn, I thought I owed it to him—and myself—to say that, for years, when he was the foremost black person presenting black characters and telling black stories, I thought Tyler Perry's films and shows made my life harder.

"So did a lot of people," Perry said, calmly, after I told him how I'd felt. "Which is surprising to me. Let me tell you what took me aback about that, when people were like, 'How dare you put fat black people on television, these are caricatures, these are stereotypes'—I was so offended because my aunt's fat. My mother's fat. My cousins are fat. People who are like, 'How dare you—these harken back to Mammy, *Amos 'n' Andy*.' I would hear all these things, and I would go, *hmmm*." When *Amos 'n' Andy* is mentioned, it's usually code for minstrelsy, but Perry disagrees. In fact, he thinks the real shame was not that black actors played roles on *Amos 'n' Andy*, but what happened to them later, when they lost work after the NAACP boycotted the TV show and it was canceled.

It comes down to the question of who gets to decide what's good for black people. Should all kinds of blackness be shown, or should its representation be curated? To Perry, no one should have the authority to make that call. To others, however, there is a clear line between what's good for "us" and what isn't. Much of the backdrop of the intellectual debates between scholars like Booker T. Washington and W. E. B. Du Bois came down to this, too, whether good fortune and success is dependent on some approval from whites, as well as on using a group of select blacks to represent the whole. We're a century removed from those thinkers—but in some ways, we're still debating those ideas, and Tyler Perry's work is at the center of it.

When you talk to someone in Perry's inner circle, it's difficult to separate the objective from the subjective. What makes this especially difficult is that many of the people in his inner circle happen to be heroic black figures. Perry picked two women to be the godmothers of his now-one-year-old son, Aman: Oprah and Cicely Tyson. In no way would you expect a godmother to give you an unbiased opinion of her godson's father, but when one of them is Cicely Tyson, you have to at least listen.

"He has been one of the greatest blessings to us as a race of people, in terms of what he's done for us. There are people in the business that never dreamed that they would have an opportunity to be on the stage, to be on the film, to be on television. And look where they are," she told me. "And you have to say, if it were not for him, they wouldn't be."

The way Oprah and Tyson speak about Perry is very protective, both motherly and sisterly, and neither thinks he's getting his just due. Never in my life had I thought of Perry, this massively successful man, as an underdog. You think about Oprah and Tyler and their money and their jets—not Oprah and Tyler as *people*, who in some ways haven't abandoned their roots and original audiences. So when you look at Perry, and the surface-level polarity between him and his audience, it's easy to think he's preying on this vulnerable, lower-class group by feeding them this lowbrow comedy.

There's also the other option, however, which is that *these are his people*. His audience is the group he still identifies with and feels part of and sees the humanity of, in a way both Hollywood and a sizable chunk of the American public do not understand. It's an audience who doesn't see this as fringe entertainment, an audience who sees this as the best entertainment, the only entertainment.

Perry, though, doesn't see this argument as being about race so much as it is about class. "In some parts of the country, the audience is 60 percent white. And then I went to El Paso, and it was 60 to 70 percent Latino. And then I realized it's not even about race as much as it is about stories that people can relate to," he told me. "I know for a fact that a lot of my audience cannot afford to just get in the Volvo and go to a therapist and spend the day off and go to the spa," he said. "The laughter and the dress and all of that stuff, it's just the anesthetic to say, 'Are you numb now?' Let's talk about some real issues," like the relationship between a mother and her daughter, like drugs, like what's behind infidelity. "There are so many people that society says their stories don't matter because they're poor."

In other words, he still feels like an outsider, no matter how much money he's worth. It's almost as if his work is a purposeful way never to become a part of the group he loathes the most: the elite. "It is unfair for black people to say, 'Carry my story in your story—show me in your story,'" he says. "And for people to say that they're stereotypes of black people, that's bullshit—it's offensive. These are real versions of us. And every one of us has the right to tell our own story."

Last year he played a cameo role in the latest *Star Trek* film, "Just to see what that world was like. What do you spend $200 million on, with a film? I can't wrap my brain around that one. There's so much waste in Hollywood."

He laughs again. "That's the great thing about being in Atlanta. People there just do the work. It's not all about the pretense, the other stuff."

Tyler Perry Is a Ninja in His Own Right, Talks Fatherhood and Going against Stereotype in New Film

Sandra Varner / 2016

From the *Jackson Advocate*, June 9, 2016. Reprinted by permission.

Turtles unite and save the world or so is the rallying cry of Michelangelo, Donatello, Leonardo, and Raphael: the beloved masked heroines lovingly known as the Teenage Mutant Ninja Turtles, out of the shadows, to right the wrongs of evildoers. Ever the stalwart defender of justice this sequel introduces a few new villains determined to annihilate the turtles. One such foe is mad scientist Baxter Stockman with Tyler Perry cast.

Perry says of his role in *Teenage Mutant Ninja Turtles 2*, "The thing I love most about this character is that he does all the work, but he's completely ignored and underserved. I can relate to that, growing up as an underdog, so I immediately sparked to him. The opportunity to play a mad scientist who becomes even madder was a lot of fun. He starts off as a not so bad guy but becomes one of the worst guys."

Talk2SV: Just can't box you in . . . Every time I think I know where you're going in this business you surprise me. Here you are, part of this beloved film franchise, in a role unlike any I've seen you portray. How did this come about?
Tyler Perry: First of all, when they (filmmakers) called and asked if I wanted to do it, I thought about my year-and-a-half old son. In a few years he'll be able to see this film. So definitely, I wanted him to have another opportunity to see Dad doing something else . . . now, with the Turtles. I thought that would be pretty cool.

Talk2SV: How is it seeing the world through your son's eyes?
Perry: It's beyond moving—the world is very different for me now—everything I do is different, everything I say is different; how I treat myself, where I go, what

I eat, how I exercise. It's all motivated by wanting to be around for him (Aman) especially having waited so late to have him even though he was a total surprise. He really has changed my life.

Talk2SV: You are a force in this business, a leader who knows what he wants, and a veritable change agent. On the flip side, where is the kid in you? How do you relate to the Ninja Turtles and to your son?

Perry: I am a big kid—forever a kid—I'm just in a big grown man's body. To see my life through his eyes is really exciting. Every day I wake up and see him I know that everything's all right in the world.

Talk2SV: We've come to know you as one of the hardest-working men in show business. How does one evolve from that identity?

Perry: My son is changing me; he's making me slow down. Before he was born I didn't take breaks and worked all the time. Now I build in longer breaks: instead of taking two weeks off it's a month off or two months off or three months off, and we'll build that into the schedule throughout the years. I can put in eighteen hours a day working really, really hard for months at a time, then take those breaks where we go away and do nothing.

Talk2SV: Switching gears a bit, yours is a very unique perspective in this business. Specifically, you're not only a filmmaker; you also own a successful film studio. When hired as an actor, how do you switch gears?

Perry: When you know you've been hired to do a job and you're being paid to do that job it is very important that you do it and to the best of your ability. You go in and give them everything they are asking for, give them everything they want; it's not your ship. It's not your show. If you wanted it to be [your] show you shouldn't have signed on for it. I come to a job from a total place of surrender when I walk on to somebody else's set.

Talk2SV: Basically, you're describing your work ethic.

Perry: Well, I appreciate that.

Talk2SV: When this film franchise began (*Ninja Turtles*), the success of it blew everybody's mind; these characters were widely embraced. You are no stranger to the impact that fictional characters can have, given your iconic Madea character. What does it tell us about the way we live vicariously through these characters?

Perry: For kids to endear these characters (*Ninja Turtles*) in the way they have is why this franchise is still around. My hope is what this says to all of us is the message conveyed to accept yourself for who you are. No matter where you are, no matter where you come from, you are special. I think it is a great message for kids, and I think that's the impact it can have on all of us—that who we are and what we are is enough.

Talk2SV: How would you describe the heart of the Teenage Mutant Ninja Turtles?
Perry: I think the heart of the Turtles, though they are fun, clumsy, pizza-loving teenagers is their intention. Their intention is always good.

Talk2SV: How would you describe your character in this film?
Perry: Baxter Stockman is a mad scientist who is a bit crazy but also very misunderstood. He is a very nice guy though nobody thinks he is a nice guy. He's a nerd, but he's fun.

Talk2SV: Something tells me there may be a little nerd inside of you.
Perry: (Laughter) Stop it . . . there is a little bit. I geek out about a few things; you start talking about airplanes and engineering, I'm right there with you.

Talk2SV: Have you taken flying lessons?
Perry: I did. I got my license.

Talk2SV: Does that mean you have like 10,000 hours?
Perry: No. You can get them with forty hours believe it or not. But I don't fly anymore because of my son. If you don't fly much then you're not very good at it. I don't have time to do it a lot. Until I can retire and can do it every day, all day, that's when you become very good. You also have to be a weatherman to really be good at it, know what clouds are and what you're looking at especially if your plane does not get above storms. Because of my son I don't fly anymore.

Talk2SV: And it was just that easy to let it go?
Perry: I started flying because I had a fear of flying. I wanted to learn more about planes. When my son was born, it was OK. Then I asked myself, "If you are over the fear what are you doing up here in a single engine plane for four people?"

Talk2SV: Again, just when I think I've got you pegged. What then, for you, is surprising about your adaptability? You live a 360-degree existence.
Perry: I never think about it. I haven't even thought about it being different degrees. I just don't feel like I'm in a box and don't feel like I belong in a box. If there's something I want to do I'm going to try it whether it works or not. I'm going to know that I gave it my best.

Talk2SV: So is it safe to say that fear is no longer a part of your reality or a lens through which you view things?

Perry: Whatever I'm afraid of, whatever is bothering me, I try to face it, to stare it down so I can get past it. I don't want anything holding me back.

Talk2SV: The city of Atlanta owes you much.

Perry: Do they?

Talk2SV: I'd say so.

Perry: I think I owe Atlanta a lot. It's been home, and it's been wonderful. Had I not seen people do well there I don't think that I would have been able to do all that I've done.

Talk2SV: Do you see yourself moving away from Atlanta at any point?

Perry: No. I have houses in other places, but Atlanta is home. It always will be home. It was the promised land for me; it was the place where I felt I could do well and now I have.

Talk2SV: Whenever I share with others that our interviews are more like conversations, sometimes I see their eyes well up. There is a kinship that you've established with total strangers through your work. Do you feel any undue pressure from that visceral connection?

Perry: No, because it's real. I'm just being myself, it's genuine, and I'm just doing what I do every day. All of my life I've tried to maintain and stay true to myself. To have strangers walk up to me smiling and laughing because of something they've seen me do on stage or in film makes me feel good, you know.

Talk2SV: Yes, I do. A couple of years ago you had a positive impact on my nephew when you shook his hand.

Perry: That's great to hear.

Interview: Tyler Perry Talks *Love Thy Neighbor, The Haves and the Have Nots,* and His Process from Page to Screen

Aramide A. Tinubu / 2016

From IndieWire.com, January 12, 2016. Reprinted by permission.

I've personally never felt that characters of African descent should be inherently good, educated, or of a particular caliber in order to be presented in film and on television. In my opinion, that is an argument of past centuries, when the narrative of black Americans on screen may have needed a particular sort of trajectory. I also feel that everyone has a right to tell their stories, but I don't feel that these stories should be mediocre or inherently stereotypical, which is why I often find the work of Tyler Perry extremely problematic. Still, despite my criticisms and the criticisms of others, Perry has carved out a prolific path for himself in the entertainment industry. From his stage plays to his body of films and now with four shows on Oprah Winfrey's OWN Network, including *Love Thy Neighbor* and *The Haves and the Have Nots,* which premiered last week to over three million viewers, it's clear that his audience is always eager to tune in.

At a recent press event for *The Haves and the Have Nots* and *Love Thy Neighbor,* Tyler Perry, as well as some of the casts from both series, including John Schneider, Angela Robinson, Patrice Lovely, and Palmer Williams sat down to talk about the success of the shows, Perry's writing process, and being a part of OWN Network. Shadow and Act was there to take it all in. Here are some of the highlights.

On the Evolution of Both *The Haves and the Have Nots* and *Love Thy Neighbor*

Tyler Perry: What's amazing about this is that we are about to cross one hundred episodes for both of these shows. What's so great about it is that you start one way, but the characters dictate where they want to go and how they want to go. If you look at a show when it first starts, you go, "Hm . . . how is going to go?" but by the tenth episode, you see the characters start to gel, and you really start to believe them. That's what has happened with both of these shows. By episode fifteen we had settled in. I think at this point in both the shows, the characters have evolved and the show has evolved. With Veronica (Angela Robinson, *HAHN*) having one or two lines in the first show, I didn't know she was going to turn out to be this character, but I love the madness of it. I love the insanity of it.

On the Writing Process

TP: I've said this before; I don't have a writer's room. I write all of the shows myself. Ninety-one episodes a season, I'm sitting at the computer writing, writing, and writing. I want the voice to be authentic, so the audience is hearing from me and not other writers. There are a lot of other shows on the air that are fantastic shows, but they have writer's rooms. The people that we love the most only write one or two episodes a season. What's great about it when you're writing for actors like this who are tremendously talented, you can throw anything at them. I sit in a room, and as I'm sitting at the computer I can hear these characters talking. The only thing that is difficult for me is to force one show out of my head so that Eddie doesn't sound like Joe, or that Mama Hattie doesn't sound like Angela, which in a way they kind of do. If you look at the characters themselves and the shows themselves they are very different, and I don't think people really give credit to how different each show is. The pleasure that I take is being at work for the actual characters themselves. So, the minute that they stop talking we have a problem.

On Branding "Tyler Perry Presents"

TP: Very early on when I started doing these plays and live shows, I was traveling from city to city, and there were a million shows out there. And I wanted to step out among it. So I started putting my name above the title. I remember getting to a city and talking to one of the promoters because my name wasn't on the marquee, and we had this argument about it. He said, "Who do you think you are?" Even then, when nobody knew my name, I had this idea to build a brand, and if you're going to build a brand then people have to recognize that brand, and when they see that brand, people have to get what they expect from that brand. For example, when you buy Coca-Cola you don't taste Pepsi. So that's what it's always been about for me. The "Tyler Perry Presents" has never been about ego; it's never been about look at me. It's about the fact that I want this brand to be identified with this kind of entertainment.

Palmer Williams: Also, it's proper etiquette in theater to put the author's name first.

On the Energy on Set between the Casts of the Various Shows

Patrice Lovely: We have the most fun because it's like Tyler handpicked each and every one of us. It's like he knew our spirits, he knew we would gel, and that's exactly what happened. On script and off script, we have a ball. We enjoy what we do. Even when we're on vacation we're running lines; we just enjoy each other's time. That's why it's so awesome onscreen.

Angela Robinson: *The Haves and the Have Nots* is the same way, and we also really enjoy the cast of *Love Thy Neighbor*. We have a great time together when we are together. We go out, and we just really, really love one another. We are there for the highs and lows of one another's lives; when there are losses, we show up for each other. I believe when it's that kind of thing, it really starts from the top. Tyler Perry promotes that at the studio, and we all just fall in line. We all love one another a whole lot, and you can feel that love when you come to the studio.

John Schneider: It's also hard work, but it's wonderful hard work. I liken it to doing a *New York Times* crossword puzzle with a sharpie. You are committed to whatever the task is at hand. We do go out and have a wonderful time before we start a season and after we finish a season, but during, there is no time. We work a lot of hours.

On the Filming Structure at Tyler Perry Studios

TP: A show like *Scandal*, or a show like *Empire* takes a week and a half to shoot one episode. Their budget is almost five times what we have to spend on an episode. We shoot an episode in a day and a half, so we are moving nonstop. We have to come to set ready to go, that's why I love these people, and that's why I love working with theater actors and people who have been around this a long time. We all come together to do this, and they all get it right away. And for the sitcoms, they are doing three and four episodes in two days. It's a different kind of experience because in Hollywood, a sitcom takes seven days to shoot. I just started a whole different system. I went out to LA, and I saw the way things were done. And I thought, There is another way to do this without killing everybody. I think we've managed to do it very well.

On Celebrities and Social Responsibility

TP: For Black Lives Matter and those kinds of issues, I will say this: I love to have a more intimate fight when it comes to helping people and those kinds of situations. There was a man named Terrence Williams, and a man named Felipe Santos that I've been fighting for years. They were put into the back of a deputy's squad car, the deputy's name was Steve Calkins, and both of them disappeared. One was a Mexican immigrant, and the other was a black man with a history of incarceration. No one would ever give Mr. Williams's mother any press when she would try to find out what had happened to them. So I prefer to be on the frontlines of things that move me in that way. I think it's just as powerful as being a part of, like, Black Lives Matter. But what's important to me is that someday these two men that disappeared almost fourteen years ago now, have a voice from someone like me who can speak up for them. As far as issues like the Black Lives Matter movement appearing on the shows, I shoot too fast to stay current of what's going on. The shows are already done for 2016; we're working on 2017 now. So we're that far ahead in how we shoot, and it's very difficult for me to be timely in my messages. I'm not a social media person; I don't know what's going on unless somebody tells me. I write and work so much that people have to stop me and say, "Did you know this happened?" That's how I like to live my life because I'd rather focus on the good that I'm trying to put out versus everyone else's heartache and hardship.

On Keeping the Faith

TP: For me, there is a guiding compass that just lives inside of me. Every time I've gone against it, something bad has happened. As long as I stay in line and honor it, it has really been life changing. That is the way I have written these shows, and that is the place where I write these shows from. If you look at *The Haves and the Have Nots*, I didn't want to write a show where everyone is great and wonderful and perfect. I wanted to write it so that you're not really sure who the haves are. You look at Hanna and you see that she doesn't have much, but she has great faith. The Christians were having a fit because Hanna is so all over the place, but she's so real. She represents such a real version of a Christian. I couldn't make her too perfect so that nobody would be able to relate to her. She represents that Christian that falls short, that makes mistakes, that has to repent, that has to pray hard for forgiveness. I don't know one Christian that can't relate to that, so for me it's my compass that is leading me to whatever is truth, whatever is right, and that's the path I'm supposed to go down.

PL: I think I just kind of stay in tune to everything. I don't do a lot of TV, I just do a lot of meditating, I listen to a lot of music, and I do a lot of outside stuff. I think that's what keeps me grounded.

JS: I've always believed that God designs us to do something very specific for his purpose. When you start to fail is when you think God has designed you to do something for your purpose. It's not your purpose; it's not about you. What are you? What are you designed to be? It's important to me to always check whether I am operating within my design, my specific design. It's a very specific design; there are as many designs as they are people. So the trap is to look at somebody else's design and say, "I want to be more like that," because that's not what it's about.

TP: This speaks to my shows and how I write. People say, "Well, Tyler, why aren't you doing this or using this kind of person? Why do your characters have to look like this?" All of that speaks to what John just said. As an individual, you don't have to conform to what everybody else thinks. You don't have to conform to what everybody thinks success should look like; it has to be true to you. I'm not interested in doing *Star Wars*. It's an amazing movie, but that's not my gift. I tell the stories that I tell that relate to the people who love what I do. That is the place and the path that I know I am supposed to be on. The minute I try and go do something else, it will be amazing to watch how quickly that doesn't work.

AR: I've always prayed, "God show me my purpose; what would you have me do?" I believe that purpose from a young age was acting; that's what I wanted to do. I realized that my purpose would lead to my service. So whatever I do as an actor I have to serve though that. My mantra every day is "How can I be of service to you God? How can I use what you've given me?" Sometimes you don't know about it, sometimes these are things you would never hear about, but we are servicing others.

PW: Just coming from humble beginnings and not feeling like I knew where I was going to end up, I still feel like I'm only 40 percent of where God has me to go. I know that your gifts and your talents are what got you there, but your character keeps you there. And that's why I want to be a man of great character.

Choosing to Film in Atlanta

TP: In New Orleans growing up, Hurricane Katrina blew the roof off of the poverty that was there. So when I got to Atlanta for the first time, I saw black people doing well. They were taking their kids to restaurants and theaters and things that we had never done growing up. So that's why it's so important for me to have the studio right in the heart of Atlanta. I'll never forget when President Obama came to the studio to do a fundraiser back in 2012. When he drove that police motorcade down the blocked-off streets, I got a chance to see the faces of all of those brown children looking and waving their flags. I knew they would never have had that experience had the studio not been in that place. I saw the hope.

On Oprah Winfrey and OWN

TP: The biggest thing for me is that when I was watching *The Oprah Winfrey* show at eighteen or nineteen years old, and she said, "Its cathartic to write things down," I had to go and look up what *cathartic* means. So, I took that and I learned and I started writing. Adding twenty-something, thirty-something years to that, having the opportunity to be on her network and writing shows for her, that is one of the most awe-inspiring things ever. I couldn't even write that story and to also be in this situation where I have four shows on the network that are doing really well. I want to set the narrative straight. If it had not been for Oprah leaving her show and sitting in as the CEO and putting the right people in place that were needed to make the network work and become successful, had it not been the power of Oprah, the advertisers would have left long before I even got there. It was the power of Oprah that saved the network and turned it around, and it is the business sense of Oprah to say, "Come do this for my network." So that is the true narrative. Yes, we have great ratings, but Oprah herself has set that network on the right path. She is the wind that is pushing it in the right direction.

PL: I think I'm just excited. I love Tyler Perry, I love Oprah, and I appreciate everything. The fact that he took the cast of *Love Thy Neighbor* there, I'm just overjoyed. I say that wherever he leads I'm going to follow.

AR: I think we all just hit the jackpot here, having the opportunity to work for the OWN Network. I have had the pleasure of doing *The Color Purple* on Broadway that Oprah produced. Knowing she was producing it gave us all this comfort just knowing we were all well cared for. Fast-forward years later and having this opportunity to work with both Oprah and Tyler Perry, I just felt like I was in the best hands.

PW: I'm very excited. I have the two greatest bosses you can have in the entertainment industry. I get to go to work only thirty-five miles away from my home. I work with one of the most prolific writers of this generation, and I get to go home and take my son to baseball practice. I get to be in Hollywood in Atlanta. I get do all of that because this gentleman has allowed me to fulfill my dreams through his vision, so I can't be nothing but excited.

JS: I have had the great fortune of being on television since 1978. So I've seen a lot of changes. I came from a three-network world, and then cable came in. And then the Internet came in. Even when I was on *Smallville*, it was frightening to know that the fate of a television show and the fate of all of the people on it, their livelihoods, and their ability to be able to able to care for their families were in the hands of people who really had no vested interest in the show. Now to be doing a show like *The Haves and the Have Nots* and being able to play a character that is so delightfully wickedly wrong, I know that my fate with regards to the show is in the hands of two people who are incredibly invested. They're not just invested emotionally, spiritually, and financially, but we know them, we work with them. Yes, we work for them, but it feels like we're all in together. And we're all enjoying tremendous success that is shared with us. That's a completely foreign experience to me.

Tyler Perry Encourages Fans to Use Their God-Given Talents to Change the World in 2017

Christine Thomasos / 2016

From www.christianpost.com, December 25, 2016. Reprinted by permission.

Tyler Perry is encouraging fans to cultivate the gifts they've received from God so they can be a blessing to others and transform the world for the better in the New Year.

"I couldn't help but to think about all of us who have gifts inside of us that are tucked away and hidden. Gifts that we have never used, gifts that have been given by God, gifts that are special, gifts that can not only change your life but the world," Perry wrote on Facebook earlier this month.

"Yet we leave them hidden, tucked away in the corners of our souls. As you leave 2016 and enter into 2017, why not commit to searching your soul for all of your gifts, even the hidden ones, and begin to use them, no matter what people say, no matter who judges you for it and no matter what people think?"

The screenwriter, director, producer, and actor with successful theatrical and film productions, went on to encourage people to use their gifts to impact others.

"Use the gifts that God has given you to help spread some hope and love and joy to this world. Boy, do we need it," he wrote before extending well wishes to fans for the Christmas holiday. "Merry CHRISTmas and a Happy New Year to you all. Thank you for an amazing 2016."

Perry became a father to his first child on November 30, 2014. And before his son was born, the entertainment mogul admitted that he struggled to find happiness during the Christmas season since his mother died in December 2009.

"This is the first Christmas in the past five years that I've been able to find joy. You see, my mother died December the eighth five years ago, and no amount of Christmas lights could replace the light that she was to me," Perry wrote to his fans on Facebook in 2014. "But this year, in spite of myself, God gave me another light to shine in my heart right beside hers. God thank you!"

He went on to share a video of a song from his play titled, *A Madea Christmas*, about Jesus.

"I wanted to dedicate this song to you this holiday season. It's from my play *A Madea Christmas*, and I love this song so much that I wanted to share it," he wrote. "It's about Mary, the mother of Jesus, but as you listen to it, you can see that it can be about any parent. You never know who God has put into your home to raise."

When he is not personally giving messages of hope to fans on social media, Perry has used his famous fictional character Madea to introduce people to Christian values.

"What I found in plays is that this character—as irreverent as she is—is very disarming. She makes you very comfortable," Perry previously told CBN. "So what I've used her as is as a tool to get people to laugh and relax so that I can talk about God, talk about faith, mention the name Jesus in my films.

"I've seen lots of people who don't go to church, who have no concept of God, who have never really thought about it, begin to change their lives because of something that was said in the film or something the character invited them to see."

Tyler Perry—*Acrimony* and Building on the Success of Madea

Trevor Noah / 2018

From *The Daily Show with Trevor Noah,* March 26, 2018. Reprinted by permission.

Trevor Noah: Please welcome Tyler Perry.
Tyler Perry: Why, why the hell did it take so long for me to be invited here, man?

TN: What do you mean, why did it take so long? You are Tyler Perry. You are an extremely busy person. You have twenty films under your belt; you have twenty plays. You have a production studio.
TP: Oh, I see.

TN: Yeah. You have a lot of things going on at the same time. You are extremely successful. When you started off, when you were doing your first Madea, did you think it was going to get to this? Did you think one day Madea would gross $500 million dollars?
TP: Hell no, or I wouldn't have done it. [laughter]

TN: You sound like Trump with the presidency now.
TP: No, no, wouldn't do the presidency. No, no, because that's really freaking annoying for a guy to be in that costume and doing that for that long.

TN: People love it though.
TP: They love it, but. . . .

TN: You know people love it. It's like people love it, and people love trashing it at the same time. But, like, Madea has this thing where—I've been in a movie watching Madea with people, and you cannot help but cheer when she starts beating a man's ass on the screen. You'll be like "Madea! Madea! Madea!" Then she starts beating someone; you're like, "Yeah!" You get into it.

TP: Go get Donald Trump, Madea, go get Donald. Yeah. I get it. I get it. I get it. I get it.

TN: That's exactly what you think it is.

TP: I get it.

TN: But it's blown up in so many different ways. Did you always see yourself as a business man? Or was it something that organically grew from Tyler Perry writing and directing, Tyler Perry producing, Tyler Perry. Did you envision this as a mogul or as something you became in time?

TP: Totally in building a brand. I approached it from building the brand. The artistry wasn't that important in the beginning. That's why I'm so excited about *Acrimony* being my first time actually expressing art. *For Colored Girls* and this one I feel like I'm really expressing an artistic side of me. But no, I was focusing on the business because I had a plan. I wanted to own a studio. I had things I wanted to do, and I wanted to serve my audience well so they could allow me to do this. And they have.

TN: That's interesting that you went to the business side first to enable you to then do the passion projects. *Acrimony* is a story that touches on so many topics that I think everyone can relate to. It's love gone wrong; it's people you know questioning each other. It's cheating or not cheating. Where do you get these stories from? What life are you living? Because this is like a theme I've noticed whenever you put pen to paper.

TP: I'm a counselor to a lot of my friends, and a lot of my friends have gone through this. What fascinated me about writing this story is that we were . . . I would hear her story, and I would hear his side. And then they weren't the same. I thought, Why don't I write a movie where two people are telling their dueling stories and let the audience decide who's telling the truth.

TN: I like the idea that you're sitting there and your friends are like, "and then my heart was broken" and you're like, "your heart was broken . . . say it again?" (as he pretends to be writing on a pad).

TP: Good line, good line right there. That's right, that's right, so don't call me if you have an issue.

TN: Do your friends ever watch the movies and then, I can picture people at the cinema, and then turning and looking at you?

TP: I don't watch it with them. I just show up at the premiere and say, "Okay y'all enjoy. I'll be over here."

TN: *Acrimony* is not just a cool story. You have an amazing cast as well. Taraji P. Henson starring in the movie. She's been a blowout star. What's it like working with her?

TP: Crazy! Taraji's really great because [speaks in a British accent] she's not one of those actresses so deep into every scene, every moment that I must concentrate and focus for hours before I can go on [ends accent]. No. She's not that at all. She does the scene. She'll be deep, she'll be in tears, and the next minute, I'll say, "Cut." And she'll say "Okay. I need some crab legs and some wine. Where are we going for dinner," kind of thing.

TN: She can flip it like that?

TP: Just like that. [speaks in a British accent] The deep thespians are really troubling like that. I can't hardly work with them all [ends accent].

TN: I think you'd be good. You should do that. Madea goes to Stratford. To be or not to be, mm hm.

TP: [In Madea's voice] To be or not to be at all. There it is.

TN: The studios in Atlanta are something everybody speaks about when they go to Atlanta. I remember when I went there and we're driving past. And I said, "What's that?" and someone said, "That's Tyler Perry's movie studios." And I was like "Ha ha, that's funny," and he was like "No, seriously, that's Tyler Perry's studios." You have built a movie studio that I now believe is bigger than Warner Brothers, and you are still building the studio. And, on top of that, which is really amazing, I—correct me if I'm wrong—believe this may be the first wholly black-owned movie studio in America.

TP: Yeah, yeah, that's true.

TN: That's a big deal for many reasons, but why do you feel it is so important for you to own your own studio and have a black-owned studio?

TP: There's an amazing thing that's happening right now. Everybody's getting a chance to tell their stories. Lisa Raye, Donald Glover, *Black Panther*, you've got all of these great things happening, but ownership is the key to make sure that longevity stays. I own everything. I would not sell a script. I would not sell a film. I would not sell a TV show. Nothing. I own it all. And to own a studio and to have *Black Panther* be shot there, which part of it was, and other movies be shot there. It's really, really phenomenal because ownership is the key to generational wealth, generational changes, and I think that's what we need to learn as people of color.

TN: That's amazing man. You've done a big thing. You've made a lot of money doing it. Is there one thing that money has changed in your life that you would never want to let go of? Is there something where you go, something benign—but where you go, like, you've got money, but, is there this one thing that I want to stay rich for?
TP: Yes.

TN: What is it?
TP: Just to not have to fly on a commercial plane is really cool. I know it's not a small thing, but it's really cool. Why are you looking at me like that?

TN: I thought you were going to be like—Madagascar grapes.
TP: No, no, no, just to . . .

TN: Fly on my own plane, it's a small thing I enjoy, so it's just you on a plane. Your own plane?
TP: Don't act like you don't do the same thing, buddy.

TN: But I have people because we are going to a comedy festival. Do you, like, sometimes go sit in the other seats and play other characters? You got to do that sometimes to make the plane feel full.
TP: You'd be very happy to know that tomorrow there'll be twelve people on the plane.

TN: Oh no, that's different; otherwise, you be like, Man, this plane is nice. And then you go around and say, like, "Oh Madea, oh, this plane is nice."
TP: That's good, that's good, man. That's rich, that's rich.

TN: Thanks so much for being on the show. *Acrimony* will be in theaters March 30. Congratulations for what you are doing. We love Taraji P. Henson. Tyler Perry everybody!

Additional Resources

Articles

Albiniak, Paige. "Once He Got Going, Nothing Could Stop Him." *Broadcasting & Cable*, January 26, 2009.

Aldridge, Leah. "Mythology and Affect: The Brands of Cinematic Blackness of Will Smith and Tyler Perry." *Spectator: The University of Southern California Journal of Film and Television* 31(1), (2011): 41–47.

Als, Hilton. "Mama's Gun: The World of Tyler Perry." *The New Yorker* (April 26, 2010): 68–72.

Ballin, Sofiya. "Tyler Perry on Why We Need Madea More than Ever." *Philadelphia Inquirer*, October 18, 2016.

Barnes, Brook. "Madea Takes a Break, and Tyler Perry Gets Serious." *The New York Times*, C 1 (2010).

Benzie, Mike. "Media Mogul Tyler Perry Never Stops." *Atlanta Journal-Constitution*, February 11, 2008.

Block, Alex B. "Tyler Perry, Inc." *The Hollywood Reporter*, February 9, 2009, 24–26.

Bonner, Joseph. "Tyler Perry: A Story of Triumph." *Legend Men's Magazine*, July 27, 2018.

Bowles, Scott. "Tyler Perry Holds On to His Past." *USA Today*, September 10, 2008.

Brown, Carolyn M. "No More Madea: Tyler Perry to Stop Filmmaking, Focus on OWN Projects." Black Enterprise.com, February 2, 2017.

Brown, Jamie F. "Tyler Perry on Another Level." *Sister 2 Sister*, April 2006.

Buggage, Edwin. "Tyler Perry: An Inspirational Journey to Greatness." *Data News Weekly*, October 18, 2017.

Carey, Tamika L. "Take Your Place: Rhetorical Healing and Black Womanhood in Tyler Perry's Films." *Signs: Journal of Women in Culture and Society* 39, no. 4 (2014): 999–1021.

Carter, Kelley L. "Tyler Perry: Playing by His Own Rules." *Crisis* (2010).

Cartier, Nina. "Black Women On-Screen as Future Texts: A New Look at Black Pop Culture Representations." *Cinema Journal* 53, no. 4 (2014): 150–57.

Cavanaugh, Tim. "Madea Does America." Reason.com, March 5, 2009.

Cavernelis, Dennis. "Tyler Perry's Journey to Forgiveness: Healing Old Wounds." *Drum*, September 14, 2017.

Chen, Gina Masullo, Sherri Williams, Nicole Hendrickson, and Li Chen. "Male Mammies: A Social-Comparison Perspective on How Exaggeratedly Overweight Media Portrayals of Madea,

Rasputia, and Big Momma Affect How Black Women Feel about Themselves." *Mass Communication and Society* 15:1, 2012.

Christian, Aymar J. "Understanding the Tyler Perry Phenomenon." *Visual Inquiry*, April 13, 2010.

Christian, Margena. "Tyler Perry: Meet the Man behind the Urban Theater Character Madea." *Jet*, December 1, 2003.

Christian, Margena. "Tyler Perry: Sky Is the Limit for 'Madea' Creator with New Movie, Upcoming Book, and TV Show." *Jet*, February 27, 2006, 32–38.

Clark, Brent. "Tyler Perry: Mediocrity Making Millions." In *Secular Morality: Rhetoric and Reader*, edited by Steve Cirrone. Sacramento, CA: SFC Publishing. 2015, 89–93.

Coleman, Chrisena. "Tyler Perry Reveals History of Childhood Abuse, Molestation." *New York Daily News*, October 5, 2009.

Coleman, Robin M. "Tyler Perry: 'The (Self-Appointed) Savior of Black Womanhood.'" In *Our Voices: Essays in Culture, Ethnicity, and Communication*, 5th ed. edited by Alberto Gonzalez, Marsha Houston, and Victoria Chen, 53–59. Oxford University Press, 2011.

Coleman, Robin M. "Tyler Perry and Black Cyber-Activism in the 21st Century." www.BlackCommentator.com, 2008.

Copeland, Kameron J. "From New Black Realism to Tyler Perry: The Characterizations of Black Masculinity in Tyler Perry's Romantic Storylines." *The Journal of Men's Studies* 25, no. 1 (2017): 70–91.

Corliss, Richard. "God and Tyler Perry vs. Hollywood." *Time* (March 20, 2008).

Crouch, Stanley. "Why We Line Up for Tyler Perry." *Tulsa World*, April 12, 2008.

Crouse, Edward E. "We Are Family." *Film Comment* 42, no. 2 (2006): 42–45.

Drumming, Neil. "The Gospel according to Tyler Perry." *EW.com*, February 24, 2006.

Falsani, Cathleen. "Perry Not Just Skin Deep." *Chicago Sun-Times*, February 27, 2009.

Flint, Joe. "Turner Broadcasting Tries to Make Peace with Tyler Perry." *The Los Angeles Times*, June 30, 2010.

Goldstein, Patrick." Tyler Perry: Movie King, Not Mogul." *Los Angeles Times*, February 27, 2009.

Grant, Drew. "Tyler Perry vs. Spike Lee: Let's Bring the Jews into This!" Salon.com, April 4, 2011.

Hare, Breeanna. "Tyler Perry: The Mogul outside the Machine." Special to CNN, April 6, 2010.

Harris, Cherise A., and Keisha Edwards Tassie. "The Cinematic Incarnation of Frazier's Black Bourgeoisie: Tyler Perry's Black Middle-Class." *Journal of African American Studies* 16, no. 2 (2012): 321–44.

Harrison, Theodore, III. "Tyler Perry's *Madea Goes to Jail*: Normalizing Hegemony and Stereotypes of 'Black Crime.'" *McNair Scholars Journal* 13 (2009): 107–20.

Hicks, Chris. "Tyler Perry Uses Themes Others Can't or Won't." *Deseret*. April 9, 2010.

Hira, Nadira A. "Diary of a Mad Businessman—Bringing Urban Theater to the Screen Has Made Tyler Perry a Star in Hollywood." *Fortune*. 155, no. 3 (2007): 76.

Hirshey, Gerri. "Tyler Perry's Brand-New Day." *Best Life*, April 2008, 88–93.

Ho, Rodney. "The Magic of Tyler Perry's *House of Payne*." *Atlanta Journal-Constitution*, February 9, 2008.

Holtman, Curt. "Tyler Perry Doesn't Need You because God Has His Back," *Creative Loafing*, April 7–13, 2011.

Indiewire Staff. "Lionsgate and Tyler Perry Extend Their Partnership." *Indiewire*, March 30, 2011.

Jakes, Thomas Dexter. "100 Influential People: Tyler Perry." *Time*, May 12, 2008.

Johnson, Rebecca. "Pastor Madea? Tyler Perry Says Preaching the Gospel Is 'in My Blood.'" *EEW Magazine Faith News*, October 27, 2017.

Jubera, Drew. "Tyler Perry Runs the Table." *Men's Health* 27(9) (November 2012): 125–31.

Kloer, Phil. "From Madea to Mogul," *Access Atlanta*, September 13, 2008.

Kloer, Phil. "Tyler Perry's Appeal is Becoming Universal." *The Courier-Journal*, February 24, 2006.

LaCroix, Jared William. "Tyler Perry." *The New Georgia Encyclopedia*. Retrieved February 11, 2017.

La Ferla, Ruth. "Sometimes Piety Isn't Squeaky Clean." *The New York Times*, October 14, 2007.

Lapowsky, Issie. "Tyler Perry Responds to Spike Lee's Claim that His Work Is Comparable to *Amos 'n' Andy*." *Daily News*, October 26, 2009.

Lee, Felicia. "Talking the Dream, Growing the Brand." *The New York Times*, June 6, 2007.

Lemieux, Jamilah. "An Open Letter to Tyler Perry." NPR, September 11, 2009.

Lundergaard, Erik. "The Secret to Tyler Perry's Success." MSNBC, March 1, 2008.

Lyle, Timothy. "'Still Playin' Wid Dem Barbie Dolls? Never Mind, Don't Answer That': Tyler Perry's Stage as a Lonely Place for Black Queers." *Continuum Journal* 3, no. 1 (2016): 1–14.

Lyle, Timothy. "'Check with Yo' Man First; Check with Yo' Man': Tyler Perry Appropriates Drag as a Tool to Re-Circulate Patriarchal Ideology." *Callaloo* 34, no. 3 (2011): 943–58.

McKoy, Brianna. "Tyler Perry and the Weight of Misrepresentation." *McNairs Scholars Research Journal* 5, no. 1 (2012): 127–46.

Miles, Kenneth. "From the Streets to the Stage." *Black Enterprise*, March 1, 2001.

Millner, Denene. "Perry's House Party." *Essence*, July 2007, 63.

Millner, Denene. "The Unstoppable Tyler Perry." *Essence*, August 2007, 97, 154.

Milloy, Courtland. "For Black Men Who Have Considered Homicide after Watching Another Tyler Perry Movie." *The Washington Post*, November 7, 2010.

Morris, Wesley. "The Year of Tyler Perry: Seriously America's Most Important Black Filmmaker." *Film Comment* 47, no. 1 (2011): 59–61.

Munoz, Lorenza. "The Hollywood Gospel according to Tyler Perry." *Los Angeles Times*, February 19, 2006.

Murray, Sonia. "The Talented Mr. Perry," *Essence*, February 2009, 112–17.

Nathanson, Jonathan. "Why Movie Critics Hate Tyler Perry." Priceonomics.com, November 1, 2013.

Neal, Mark A. "Tyler Perry and the Black Bible Belt." *Critical Noir*. Vibe. com (2007).

Nelson, Angela M. "Religious Rhetoric in Tyler Perry's Play *Madea's Family Reunion*." *Memphis Theological Seminary Journal* Vol. 50, March 23, 2011.

O'Brian, Conan. "Tyler Perry Interview." *Late Night with Conan O'Brien*, March 20, 2011. TBS.com.

Olsen, Mark. "Tyler Perry Puts His Faith behind, and into His Work." *Chicago Tribune*, March 4, 2015.

Parekh, Rupal. "How Tyler Perry's House of Hits Was Built." *Advertising Age* 80 (2009): 24.

Patterson, Robert J. "'Woman Thou Art Bound': Critical Spectatorship, Black Masculine Gazes, and Gender Problems in Tyler Perry's Movies." *Black Camera* 3, no. 1. (2011): 9–30.

Perrine, Unk and Stephen. "How Tyler Perry Went from Living in His Car to Commanding a $500 Million Empire." *Best Life*, April 2008.

Perry, Tyler. "The Power of Perseverance." *Guideposts*, January 2017.

Persley, Nicole H. "Bruised and Misunderstood: Translating Black Feminist Acts in the Work of Tyler Perry." *Palimpsest: A Journal on Women, Gender, and the Black International* 1, no. 2 (2012): 217–36.

Pomerantz, Dorothy. "The Amazing Tyler Perry." *Forbes*, April 21, 2011.

Pulley, Brett. "Hollywood's Maverick Mogul—Who Needs Hollywood to Become a Star? Tyler Perry Is the Best-Kept Secret in Moviemaking." *Forbes* 75 (2005).

Quinn, Eithne. "Black Talent and Conglomerate Hollywood: Will Smith, Tyler Perry, and the Continuing Significance of Race." *Popular Communication* 11, no. 3 (2013).

Reed, Ashley, and Jennifer Larson. "Madea's Middle Class: Sentimental Spaces in Tyler Perry's *Madea's Family Reunion* and *Why Did I Get Married?*" In *Sentimental Mode: Essays in Literature, Film, and Television*, edited by Jennifer A. Williamson, Jennifer Larson, and Ashley Reed, 190–210. Jefferson, NC: McFarland & Co. 2014.

Saine, KB. "The Black American's Chitlin/Gospel/Urban Show: Tyler Perry and the Madea Plays." *Theatre Symposium: A Journal of the Southeastern Theatre* (January 2005).

Slagle, Dana. "Tyler Perry Takes on TV with New Sitcom *House of Payne*.'" *Jet*, June 11, 2007.

Sperling, Nicole. "Lionsgate Nabs 11th Tyler Perry Movie." *Entertainment Weekly*. EW.com, April 28, 2010.

Stack, Tim. "Tyler on Top." *The New York Times*, June 6, 2007.

Svetkey, Benjamin, Margeaux Watson, and Alynda Wheat. "'Madea': Bad for Black America?" *Entertainment Weekly*. www.ew.com, March 17, 2009.

Thompson, Arienne. "For Tyler Perry, It's Lonely at the Top." *Houston Chronicle*, June 4, 2013.

Tillet, Salamishah. "Black Feminism, Tyler Perry Style." The Root.com. *November 11, 2010.*

Toto, Christian. "What Would Madea Say?" *The Washington Times*, March 28, 2008.

Turner, Miki. "Mad for Madea: Popular Character Isn't Only Thing Keeping Prolific Tyler Perry Busy." *Chicago Tribune*, February 24, 2006.

Turner Miki. "Tyler Perry Reveals His Secret to Success." *Today Show*. Today.com, February 12, 2007.

"Tyler Perry Studios Opening." *Jet*, October 20–27, 2008, 4, 58.

Villarreal, Yvonne. "Oprah's OWN Partners with Tyler Perry." *Los Angeles Times*, October 01, 2012.

Whitaker, Morgan. "Once Homeless, Tyler Perry's Now a Hollywood Success. Here's How." MSNBC. Msnbc.com, September 7, 2013.

White, Michael. "Filmmaker Perry Produces Profits, Smiles." *Tribune-Review/Pittsburgh Tribune-Review*, March 21, 2008.

Williams, Danielle E. "He Who Has the Gold Makes the Rules: Tyler Perry Presents 'The Tyler Perry Way.'" In *How Television Shapes Our Worldview: Media Representations of World Trends and Change*, edited by Deborah A. Macey, Kathleen M. Ryan, and Noah J. Springer, 291–306. Lanham, MD: Lexington Books, 2014.

Winfrey, Oprah. "Oprah Talks to Tyler Perry." *O, The Oprah Magazine*, December 2010: 228–38.

Wingard, Leslie E. "Gracefully Policing the Tyler Perry Phenomenon." *American Quarterly* 67, no. 4 (2015): 1251–58.

Wulandari, Meri. "The Idea of Gender Oppression over Man Domination in Tyler Perry's *For Colored Girls* Movie." Unpublished paper. State University of Surabaya.

Zeitchik, Steven. "Perry's Success Has Black Film in Fashion." Reuters.com, October 17, 2007.

Books

Asur, Omara. *Who Is Tyler Perry—Biography of an American Dream*. Kindle Book. Amazon Digital Service LLC. 2012.

Bell, Jamel Santa Cruze, and Ronald L. Jackson, eds. *Interpreting Tyler Perry: Perspectives on Race, Class, Gender, and Sexuality*. New York: Routledge. 2014.

Carey, Tamika L. *Take Your Place: The Rhetoric of Return in Tyler Perry's Films*. New York: SUNY Press. 2016.

Childs, Melvin. *Never Would Have Made It: The Rise of Tyler Perry, The Most Powerful Entertainer in Black America (and What It Really Took to Get Him There)*. Santa Cruz, CA: Touch 1 Media. 2012.

Donaldson, Catherine V. "Tyler Perry." *Encyclopedia of Word Biography*. 2006.

Fain, Kimberly. *Black Hollywood: From Butlers to Superheroes, the Changing Role of African American Men in the Movies*. Praeger Books. 2015.

Gitlin, Marty. *Tyler Perry: A Biography of a Movie Mogul*. Berkeley Heights, N.J.: Enslow Publishers. 2014.

Grimm, R. B. *Tyler Perry Unauthorized and Uncensored*. 2014.

Johnson, Brian C. *The Problematic Tyler Perry*. New York: Peter Lang. 2016.

Lee, Shayne. *Tyler Perry's America: Inside His Films*. Lanham, N.Y.: Rowman & Littlefield. 2015.

Manigault-Bryant, Le Rhonda S., Tamura A. Lomax, and Carol B. Duncan. eds. *Womanist and Black Feminist Responses to Tyler Perry's Productions*. New York: Palgrave Macmillan. 2015.

Mattern, Joanne. *Tyler Perry*. Hockessin, Del.: Mitchell Lane Publishers, 2013.

Perry, Tyler. *Don't Make a Black Woman Take Off Her Earrings*. New York: Riverhead Books. 2006

Perry, Tyler. *Higher Is Waiting*. New York: Random House. 2017.

Russworm, TreaAndrea M., Samantha N. Sheppard, and Karen M. Bowdre, eds. *From Madea to Media Mogul: Theorizing Tyler Perry*. Jackson, MS: University Press of Mississippi. 2016.

Saathoff, Evan. *Madea Lives! A Film-by-Film Guide to Loving Tyler Perry*. Kindle Book. Amazon Digital Services LLC. 2014.

Sans, Christopher. *The Courage to Laugh Out Loud: Tyler Perry, An Unofficial Examination*. Biblio-Bazaar, 2010.

Scholar, Trivia. *Terry Perry Quiz Book—50 Fascinating & Fact Filled Questions about the Greatest Filmmaker of All Time*. Kindle Book. Amazon Digital Services LLC. 2013.

Skogen, J. M. *Film*. 2015. Internet resource.

Thompson, Cliff, ed. "Perry, Tyler." *Current Biography Yearbook* 6. H. W. Wilson Co. June 2005.

The Tyler Perry Handbook: Everything You Need to Know About Tyler Perry. [United States]: Emereo Publishing. 2013.

Uschan, Michael V. *Tyler Perry*. Detroit, MI: Lucent Books. 2010.

Walker, Ben. *Tyler Perry Movies—Budget vs Box Office: Tables, Charts & Notes*. Kindle Book. Amazon Digital Services LLC. 2014.

Ward, CR, and Stephen Wilcox. *FAME: Tyler Perry*. Bluewater Productions, Inc. 2015.

Watson, Jamantha Williams. *Tyler Perry: One Man Show*. Kindle Book. Amazon digital Services, LLC. 2015.

Wright, Ellen. *From the Mind of Madea: The Biography of Tyler Perry*. Kindle Book. Amazon Digital Services LLC. 2006.

Documentaries and Video Recordings

Bonfiglio, Michael. "Visionaries: Inside the Creative Mind: Tyler Perry." Documentary. August 28, 2011.

Newman, Ray, Anthony Douglas, and Theron K. Cal. "Tyler Perry: Film Maker, Business Entrepreneur, Entertainment Mogul: The Unauthorized Story." Azure Entertainment, Inc. Video Recording. 2013.

O'Brien, Soledad. "Becoming Tyler Perry." In *Black in America2: Soledad O'Brien Reports*. Documentary, Atlanta, GA: CNN, 2009.

Interviews

Allen, Nick. "Looking for Truth: Tyler Perry on *Tyler Perry's Boo! A Madea Halloween*." Rogerebert.com, October 18, 2016.

Als, Hilton. "Tyler Perry Simplifies, Commodifies Black Life." NPR, May 12, 2010.

Ballin, Sofiya. "Tyler Perry on Why We Need Madea More than Ever." *The Philadelphia Inquirer*. Phily.com, October 18, 2016.

Cagle, Jess. "Tyler Perry: The Jess Cagle Interview." *People TV*, October 19, 2017.

Cameron, Ryan. "Tyler Perry." *The Ryan Cameron Morning Show*, September 24, 2013.

Christian, Margena. "Becoming Tyler: Bill Collector Turned Billion-Dollar Media Mogul Was Molded from Pain, Promise and Persistence." *Ebony* 63 (2008): 73–83.

Clifton, Nikki. "A Conversation with Tyler Perry." *Westside Gazette*, April 20, 2006.

Colbert, Stephen. "Tyler Perry Talks about African American Actors in Hollywood, the Upcoming Election, and His Latest Film, *Alex Cross*." *The Colbert Report*. Comedy Central, October 17, 2012.

Corden, James. "Tyler Perry." On *The Late-Night Show with James Corden*. Season 1, Episode 133, January 15, 2016.

D'Addario, Daniel. "9 Questions with Tyler Perry." Time.com, March 24, 2016.

DeGeneres, Ellen. "Tyler Perry Talks 'Madea,' Clowns and Zombies." *The Ellen Show*, October 19, 2016.

Fales-Hill, Susan. "Tyler Perry Talks Black Women, Success & Being Generous." *Essence*, November 2012.

Fallon, Jimmy. "Chicago Turned Tyler Perry into Madea." *The Tonight Show Starring Jimmy Fallon*, October 8, 2016.

Freeman, D. W. "Tyler Perry, Oprah Talk Sexual Abuse: Who Victimized Little Tyler?" CBS.com, October 22, 2010.

Goldberg, Whoopi, Candace Cameron Bure, and Joy Behar. "Tyler Perry: *Boo! A Madea Halloween*." *The View*. Season 20, episode 20, October 20, 2016.

Gross, Terry. "Tyler Perry Transforms: From Madea to Family Man." *Fresh Air*. NPR, October 15, 2012.

Guthrie, Marisa. "Tyler Perry Talks Race in Hollywood, Bill Cosby and Creative Freedom: 'I Don't Get Notes.'" *The Hollywood Reporter*, May 17, 2017.

Hall, Arsenio. "Tyler Perry Explains the Birth of 'Madea' & Why He Started Writing." *The Arsenio Hall Show*, September 4, 2014.

Hall, Tamron. "A Conversation with Tyler Perry." Special event of the television academy, Atlanta, GA, May 5, 2017.

Handler, Chelsea. "Tyler Perry Interview." *Chelsea*. Netflix, October 21, 2016.

Hare, Breeanna. "Tyler Perry: The Mogul outside the Machine." *CNN*, April 6, 2010.

Harris, Neil P. "Tyler Perry." On *Best Time with Neil Patrick Harris*. Season 1, Episode 133, January 15, 2016.

Harvey, Steve. "Tyler Perry." *The Steve Harvey Morning Show*, March 29, 2013.

Harvey, Steve. "Tyler Perry Talks Fatherhood." *The Steve Harvey Show*, April 4, 2013.

Hughes, Zondra. "How Tyler Perry Rose from Homelessness to a $5 Million Mansion." *Ebony* 59, no. 3 (2004): 86.

Johnson, Tonisha. "*Diary of a Mad Black Woman*: An Interview with Tyler Perry." Blackfilm.com, February 2005.

Kimmel, Jimmy. "Tyler Perry." On *Jimmy Kimmel Live*, February 18, 2009.

King, Gayle. "Tyler Perry Reflects on Learning from His Pain." *CBS This Morning*, November 16, 2017.

King, Larry. "Tyler Perry's Rise to Success." *Larry King Live*. CNN, February 21, 2009.

Kozlowski, Carl. "Tyler Perry Interview: Questions from Big Hollywood Writer Prompts, 'Spike Lee Can Go Straight to Hell!'" *Breitbart*, April 25, 2011.

Leno, Jay. "Tyler Perry." On *The Tonight Show with Jay Leno*. Season 22, Episode 47, December 1, 2013.

Mabrey, Vicki, and Tarana Harris. "Being Tyler Perry." Nightline. *World News Tonight*. ABC, February 21, 2007.

Martin, Michel. "Shop Talk: Tyler Perry Lashes Out at Spike Lee." NPR 22, April 2011. Interview. Special Series: Barbershop Roundtable. NPR.

McGraw, Phil. "Tyler Perry's Inspirational Interview." *The Dr. Phil Show*. CBS, May 12, 2009.

Mitchell, Elvis. "Tyler Perry Interview." *Charlie Rose*, April 18, 2006.

Morgan, Piers. "Interview with Tyler Perry." *Piers Morgan Tonight*. CNN, October 19, 2012.

Myers, Seth. "Tyler Perry." On *Late Night with Seth Myers*. Season 5, Episode 82, March 22, 2018.

Noah, Trevor. "Tyler Perry—*Acrimony* and Building on the Success of 'Madea.'" *The Daily Show*. Comedy Central, March 26, 2018.

O'Brien, Soledad. "Black in America 2: Interview with Tyler Perry." CNN.com, July 23, 2010.

Ofole-Prince, Samantha. "Tyler Perry Interview: 'I Want My Films to Be Relevant to People's Lives.'" Gospelherald.com, March 11, 2014.

Radish, C. "Tyler Perry Talks *Alex Cross*, Learning Krav Maga, Taking on Similar Roles in the Future, Fight Sequences with Matthew Fox and Reactions from Madea Fans." *Collider*, October 16, 2012. htttp://collider.com/tyler-perry-alex-cross-interview/.

Ray, Rachel. "We're Kicking off Thanksgiving Week with the One and Only Tyler Perry!" *Rachel Ray Show*. Season 12, Episode 51. Nov. 20, 2017.

Ripa, Kelly, and Ryan Seacrest. "Tyler Perry Interview." *Live with Kelly and Ryan*. ABC, October 10, 2017.

Roberts, Deborah. "Diary of a Successful Black Playwright." *World News Tonight*. ABC News, June 17, 2005.

Roberts, Robin. "Tyler Perry 'OWNS' TV." Interview, *Good Morning America*, ABC News, January 8, 2016.

Slegel, Robert. "War of Words: Tyler Perry vs. Spike Lee." Interview. *All Things Considered*, NPR, April 21, 2011.

Smiley, Rickey. "Tyler Perry Explains Why He Launched a Show with a Predominately White Cast [Exclusive Interview]." *Ricky Smiley Morning Show*, August 22, 2016.

Smiley, Tavis. "Talks with Cast Members of the New Film, *Madea's Family Reunion*: Tyler Perry, Cicely Tyson, Blair Underwood and Lyn Whitfield." *The Tavis Smiley Show*. Episode 5134, February 23, 2005.

Symmonds, Nicole. "Tyler Perry Interview." Beliefnet.com, September 2009.

Thompson, Arienne. "Tyler Perry, Lonely at the Top." *USA Weekend*, May 30, 2013.

"Tyler Perry Biography." The famouspeople.com.

Ulaby, Neda. "More than 'Madea': Tyler Perry Changes Course." *All Things Considered*. NPR, March 8, 2010.

The Talk: Tyler Perry. Season 3, Episode 31, October 22, 2012.

The View: Tyler Perry. Season 15, Episode 110, February 21, 2012.

The View: Tyler Perry. Season 17, Episode 122, March 12, 2014.

The View: Tyler Perry. Season 20, Episode 33, October 20, 2016.

The View: Tyler Perry. Season 21, Episode 142, Match 26, 2018.

Williams, Kam. "Inspired Tyler Talks about Life." *Our 2cents*. FLOW Entertainment. Retrieved October 12, 2016.

Williams, Kam, and S. Frederic. "Tyler Perry's Dynasty of Movie *Family That Preys*." *Los Angeles Sentinel* Vol. LXXVI (23), June 12, 2010.

Winfrey, Oprah. "Oprah Talks to Tyler Perry." *O, the Oprah Magazine*, December 2010, 228–38.

Winfrey, Oprah. "Tyler Perry's First Interview." *The Oprah Winfrey Show*, April 23, 2001.

Winfrey, Oprah. "Tyler Perry and Madea Interview." *The Oprah Winfrey Show*, January 27, 2006.

Winfrey, Oprah. "Tyler Perry's 10th Interview." *The Oprah Winfrey Show*, October 20, 2010.

Theses/Dissertations

Faust, Mitchell R. "Are You Getting Angry Doctor?": Madea, Strategy and the Fictional Rejection of Black Female Containment. PhD diss., University of Texas. 2014.

Fontaine, Nargis. From Mammy to Madea, and Examination of the Behaviors of Tyler Perry's Madea Character in Relation to the Mammy, Jezebel, and Sapphire Stereotypes. M.A. thesis. Georgian State University. 2011.

Hall, Terrence. From Tyler, Texas to Tyler Perry: Racial Ideology and Black Film. MA thesis, University of Georgia, 2008.

Harris, Patrice. Black Masculinity in Tyler Perry's *Diary of a Mad Black Woman*. MA thesis, University of Central Missouri. 2010.

Heartley, Alfred. M. Madea's Family History: A Critical Analysis of the Stage Plays and Films of Tyler Perry. Unpublished honors thesis. Florida State University, 2011.

Jackson, Nicole E. The Tyler Perry Effect: Examining the Influence of Black Media Images on the Black Identity. MA thesis. University of Central Florida. 2011.

Long, Jaquet. Repercussions and Shifts in Form between Ntozake Shange's Play *For Colored Girls Who Have Considered Suicide When the Rainbow Is Enuf* and Tyler Perry's Film for *Colored Girls*. Senior Independent Study Thesis. The College of Wooster. 2012. Paper 263.

Lyle, Timothy S. Check with Yo' Man First, Check with Yo' Man: Perry Appropriates Drag as a Tool to Recirculate Patriarchal Ideology. Atlanta, Ga: Georgia State University, 2009. Internet resource.

McDole, Ayondela. Fat, Black and Ugly: The Politics of Postmodern Blackness and the Millennium Mammy. PhD diss. Columbia College, 2012.

Ross, Avina Ichele. Black Feminist Discourse Analysis of Portrayals of Gender Violence against Black Women: A Social Work Dissertation. PhD diss. Virginia Commonwealth University, 2016.

Shea, Staci R. Race, Capitalism, and the Films of Tyler Perry. PhD diss., St. Cloud State University, 2011.

Williams, Danielle E. Black Public Creative Figures in the Neo-Racial Moment: An Analysis of Tyra Banks, Tyler Perry and Shonda Rhimes, 2005–2010. Scholar Works @ Georgia State University, 2012.

Index

About the Editor

Janice D. Hamlet is associate professor of communication at Northern Illinois University, where she also serves as Director of Diversity, Equity, and Inclusion for the College of Liberal Arts and Sciences. Hamlet's research focuses on the impact of diversity in the media, society, and higher education; rhetoric and public address, multicultural approaches to pedagogy; African American rhetoric and culture; and the rhetorical impact of autoethnography. She has edited additional books: *Afrocentric Visions: Studies in Culture and Communication* and *Fight the Power! The Spike Lee Reader* (with Dr. Robin Means Coleman). She has published in *Communication Quarterly*, *Communication Teacher*, *Western Journal of Black Studies*, *Journalism and Mass Communication Quarterly*, *Journal of Black Studies*, *Popular Culture Studies Journal*, and *New Directions in Teaching and Learning*. Hamlet conducts workshops on cultural competency, social activism, and various diversity-related issues. She teaches courses in intercultural communication, rhetoric, and rhetorical criticism.

Photo credit: Northern Illinois University – Institutional Communications Photography

CPSIA information can be obtained
at www.ICGtesting.com
Printed in the USA
BVHW072301230819
556701BV00002B/7/P

9 781496 824592